A Kid From Legaginney

By
Finbarr M. Corr, Ed.D

9/19/10

To John

Enjoy my journey

[signature]

FMC Press
Morristown, NJ

Cover Design by Janine Myer, Alphagraphics, Morristown NJ

Printed in the United States of America by Quebecor World Book Services, Fairfield, PA

FMC Press

ISBN 1-58570-112-2

Dedication and Acknowledgements

I wrote this book because I wanted to share humorous reflections and inspirations from my youth in Ireland and from my twenty-eight years as a Catholic priest in America. I am now married. My wife, Laurie Hutton Corr, tells her friends that it is a lot of fun being married to the "kid from Legaginney." I am sure, however, that there were times during the writing and editing of this book that she wondered about her choice. A husband who was a farmer from Kansas, where she was born, would probably have done a better job than I of leaving her alone to tend to all the things she needs to do to make her own career a success. The truth is, she was there with me all the way, very patient and mildly critical when she needed to be. That is why I am dedicating *A Kid From Legaginney* to Laurie.

I wish to thank Joan Hoffman, Cristine Farrell, and Gemma Calimeri, the volunteer typists who first helped me produce this manuscript. A special thanks is due to Dr. Ruth K. Westheimer for her very positive and encouraging Preface. Finally, I am grateful to Pierre Lehu, my book agent; Mary Woodward, for editing; Bob Woodward, for formatting; Joe Ohlandt from Temple Publishers in Morristown, New Jersey, for printing service and support; and Hellen C. Davis of Indaba, for comments and publishing advice.

Preface
by Dr. Ruth K. Westheimer

As someone whose life has taken quite a few twists and turns – from an orphan of the Holocaust to celebrity sex therapist, with many stops in between – I stand well situated to appreciate my good friend Finbarr Corr's autobiography. He only moved from Ireland to America, as opposed to my stays in Germany, Switzerland, Israel, and Paris before moving here, and he only had to deal with a change of accent instead of changes in language, but since he went from layman to celibate priest to married man, he has one up on me in that arena. And, of course, he has an entire footstool of steps on me in terms of height. But although our perspectives may be different in some respects, we share many common bonds, such as a sense of humor, a desire to help our fellow human beings, and a zest for life.

I met Finbarr at Columbia University's Teachers College. Though I am very Jewish, it pleases me no end to be around people of other religions, particularly priests. He invited me to co-teach some Pre-Cana classes, which are the courses that a Catholic couple about to be married must take before the Church will sanctify their union. For a Jewish therapist to have the opportunity of sharing this experience was rather out of the ordinary, but to be able to do this with a tall, good-looking Irish priest made it well worth the regular drives into New Jersey where Finbarr was based.

I think that my part of his story, and it is only a small part, shows you what type of guy Finbarr Corr is. He is not someone willing to be hemmed in by rules, regulations, or convention. He knew that the couples under his care would benefit from the information I could give them, and so who I was became a lot less important than what I had to offer. Of course, if I had been the notorious Dr. Ruth in those days, and not just simply Ruth Westheimer, even Finbarr might not have been able to stand the heat that my participation in his course would have caused. But you know what? I'm certain that at least he would have tried.

What this book shows, as do the books of many courageous people, is that you have to be willing to be like the turtle and stick your neck out if you want to get anywhere. So while you might laugh at the funny experiences in Finbarr's life, what I urge you to take away from reading this book is the important lesson that it doesn't matter where you're from – a large family from Legaginney, Ireland, or a small one from Frankfurt-am-Main, Germany, or Main Street, USA – you can lead a fascinating and fun-filled and rewarding life if you give it your all.

**Celebrating with his parents
after his first mass**

Legaginney House

Chapter 1

Legaginney

Legaginney House rests in a beautiful valley four hundred yards south of Potahee Mountain and the same distance from the country road. When we nine Corr kids were growing up there in the 1940s, Legaginney was usually very quiet except when local hunters were busy chasing a fox or hare through the meadows on wintry Sunday afternoons. Visitors to our home were directed to turn left up the narrow lane under the Legaginney bridge and then, forty yards up the little hill, to proceed past Bridget and Phildy McCuskers' thatched house on the right.

Unlike the visitors, we Corr kids never passed the McCuskers' house without stopping. Mrs. McCusker loved children. Not blessed with any of her own, she, for all practical purposes, had adopted the nine of us. If she decided there was something a Corr kid could do for her, that was very fortunate indeed. She praised the lucky one as the most wonderful child that went to St Michael's Church in Potahee, and she treated with a generous slice of her best currant cake. Much credit to her, she remembered all nine of our birthdays. We suspected that she never told her husband Phildy how generous she was, stuffing a half crown into our pockets, as we all knew that he was as tight as a gravedigger's lips on a frosty morning.

Visitors coming by foot from the nearby village of Ballinagh could take a shortcut over the railroad tracks and across Scott's field to the lane leading up to the farmyard and residence. The tracks were quiet most of the time, except when an occasional train flew through on its way to or from Dublin. Before crossing the tracks, we Corr kids had strict orders always to check with Miss Berrill, the gatekeeper who lived alone in a small bungalow there. Since Miss Berrill only had to close and open the gates when the infrequent train came through, she welcomed our company and loved to entertain us with stories about her seven cats and the many collectibles that filled every nook and cranny of her tiny kitchen.

In turn Miss Berrill was a frequent visitor to our house. She both admired and envied my mom Nell's talent at playing the violin and accordion. With only a bit of encouragement, she would add to Mom's rendition on the accordion by belting out a lilting Irish ballad, or could switch at a moment's notice to a parody that had us all splitting our sides with laughter. When the occasion was a going-away party for a Corr or a neighbor, she would bring us to tears as she sang "Goodbye Johnny Dear."

All of our neighbors held the Corrs in high esteem, partly because they thought we were rich and partly because Dad had three brothers in the priesthood, a source of social esteem for families in Ireland. In truth, we had very little money. Dad worked hard to put food on the table and clothes on our backs. Our meals were simple and nutritious, and most of the food was produced on the farm. Dad's cows produced the milk and his pigs provided the bacon. Mom's hens produced the eggs and chickens for our Sunday dinners. One winter Dad lost ninety percent of his cattle in a freak snowstorm, which meant that for several weeks it was rice and potatoes for the Corr family dinner.

In the fields Dad plowed and harvested the corn with horses while the rest of us worked with our bare hands. The hired man cut the turf, and we boys caught the wet sods and carried them on a wheelbarrow to where they were spread out to dry before being stacked for the winter fires. It was hard work, but it was also fun because families often worked next to each other, each cutting its own bank of turf. Since some families came a relatively long distance by horse and cart to stay for the day, a picnic atmosphere often filled the bog. Two or three people in a family would start cutting, while another family member would start a fire to cook a fine meal. By early afternoon, full of potatoes, cabbage, and boiled bacon, they would invite neighbors over for tea and biscuits. With luck, our work was done by six in the evening.

The fun of having eight brothers and sisters more than compensated for any sense of hardship. As children, we were constantly playing tricks on each other, but never in mean spirit. On Christmas Eve, my oldest brother P.Joe, with whom I shared the bed where our Christmas stockings hung, would put coal into my stocking along with the other goodies from "Santa." When I discovered the coal, I needed to laugh quietly so as not to wake my little brothers Colm and Fonsie, who were asleep in their bed nearby and already dreaming of the visit by the real Santa Claus later that night.

The neighbors didn't always appreciate our humor. Phildy McCusker got quite angry one Sunday when my brother Brendan threw a snowball down his chimney on our way home from mass. The snowball landed in Phildy's dinner as it cooked in an open pot in the fireplace. Phildy stormed out of the house, threatening to report us first to Mom and, worse still, to Dad. Brendan, the Corr kid most blessed with the blarney, apologized profusely, and, with the help of softhearted Bridget, stopped Phildy from charging down the lane and causing us belting from Dad or a sermon from Mom for "bringing shame on the Corrs of Legaginney."

The Catholic religion dominated our daily lives. Before we could walk or talk, we were socialized to think and feel that God was watching over us at every step. In practice that meant we had better obey our parents, keep the rules of the Church, and follow the priests' edicts - and not always in that order. Otherwise there would be consequences, such as spending years in Purgatory or, God forbid, in hell for all eternity. From an early age we were trained to share the Good News of Jesus Christ with the less fortunate throughout the world. Visiting missionaries would appeal to us to contribute pennies for the conversion of black babies in Africa. To make donation attractive, the priests would distribute mite boxes with a statue of a black baby perched on the top. When we deposited a coin, the little baby bobbed his head in appreciation.

By the age of seven I was already on my way to being a full-fledged missionary. I sold raffle tickets in the neighborhood at three pence each for a fictitious missionary called Noogey. In spite of my being teased and getting the nickname Noogey, I felt newly charged with a great purpose. When Mrs. McCusker asked on my tenth birthday, "What would you like to be when you grow up?" I replied without a moment of hesitation, "I want to be a priest just like my Uncle Fr. Michael in America."

At that age I had never met Uncle Mike, but he was my hero. He had served in the United States Army

4

during the First World War and been highly decorated by both the American and French governments. As a young boy I would sneak up to the parlor and look at his picture hanging over the mantelpiece. To me he was an icon. I wanted to be just like him, and even parted my hair the same way. Mrs. McCusker was not impressed, nor was she shy about expressing her feelings. She looked me straight in the eye and said, "I don't think you will be a priest like Fr. Michael. You have too much of an eye for pretty girls." As you will learn later, Mrs. McCusker was partly prophetic.

Fr. Tom, another brother of Dad's, was a pastor in New Jersey, where he died in his early thirties after an attack of appendicitis as he finished Sunday mass. The parishioners of St Lucy's Parish in Jersey City crowded their church for his funeral. The copy of the parish bulletin they sent to the Corr family in Ireland eulogized him for his devotion to the poor in Jersey City.

Fr. Larry, the third priest brother, served in Ireland and was a very big part of our lives growing up. Mom would always make a big fuss about him whenever he came to dinner or evening tea. He loved wrestling with us children and would laugh from the pit of his stomach whenever my sister Marie insisted on taking off his Roman collar to make sure it was not permanently fixed around his neck.

One highlight of growing up on a farm was that there were always lots of people around. Because labor was cheap in the forties and fifties, many farmers with large acreage had hired help that lived with the family. Of all the help that Dad brought in over the years, our favorite was Jack Murtagh. Mom and Dad loved him because he was a loyal and hard worker. We kids loved him because of the condition in which he came home on Saturday nights. Having had more than his quota of Guinness stout at Paddy Wall's pub in Ballinagh, he would swagger back up the lane drunk as a lord and singing at full throttle. In the meantime, mom's helper Mary Farrelly often had us lined up by the turf fire to dry our hair, just washed for Sunday church. None of us rushed to get off to bed because we knew that any minute Jack would appear.

As he entered, the youngest Corr child present always had the privilege of searching for the bag of sweets we knew he had hidden away in the lining of his big coat. As we feasted on the candy, Jack would entertain us with funny stories from the many places he had worked before Legaginney. We never understood why he was in such a jovial mood on Saturday night but in a really rotten mood on Sunday morning, as no adult ever took the time to explain to us that a hangover on Sunday morning was a quite a different kettle of fish.

Mary Farrelly had come to work for Mom when she was only seventeen. From the beginning, she was treated as part of the family. She slept with my sisters Eilish, Marie, and Dympna in the girls' bedroom and took a regular seat at the kitchen table for family meals. Being young herself, Mary understood the minds of children and would often participate in many of our games at night. When Mom was sick or off to town shopping or visiting relatives, Mary was our second mother, taking charge and rewarding us with a hug when we obeyed her and spanking our butts when we didn't and rightly deserved it.

I was certain that I was one of her favorites of the nine Corr children because Mary would always say,

"Finbarr is the best baby of all the Corrs." Much later I discovered that Mary loved me because when she put me in my cradle on a Sunday evening I would rock myself to sleep, leaving her free to sneak down the lane to meet her boyfriend, our neighbor Josie Beatty.

We had always worried that Mary would leave our family and go back to her own family in Clones, a town twenty miles away. One day our worst fears were realized when Mary decided that her brother Tom in Clones needed her more than the Corrs. We had a tearful parting as Mary took the bus at Miss Berrill's railroad crossing and rode away to Clones via Cavan town. But Josie Beatty loved Mary too much to let some other fellow have the chance to marry her. Every Sunday morning after early mass Josie rode his bicycle to Clones to continue courting her. Weren't we happy kids when we learned a year later that Mary and Josie were to be married and that Mary was moving back to live with Josie and his parents just up the road!

Josie's dad, old Jimmy Beatty, was central in the lives of all the people who attended St Michael's Church Potahee. The church sacristan, old Jimmy rang the church bell three times a day, calling the farmers in the valley and the housewives at home to stop whatever they were doing and pray the Angelus. We children never had trouble getting permission to visit the Beattys.

One of our biggest thrills was to climb the sixty or so steps up the mountainside to help old Jimmy ring the bells. He always carefully explained the ritual to us: "You must ring it three times and come to a full stop. The first three rings are to commemorate the three years that Jesus spent in public teaching about salvation and establishing the Christian faith. Then after a pause you ring it again for thirty three times to call in mind the years that Jesus spent as a young man working with His stepfather Joseph as a carpenter's helper."

Whether at home in Legaginney house or just hanging out with the Beattys, we had constant reminders that God and religion were the most important things in our lives. Added to that, the authoritative preaching by the priest from the altar put the fear of God not just in the hearts of us kids but in those of our parents as well. Nobody dared dream of missing Sunday mass. If for any reason, such as a bad cold, any Corr kid felt that he wouldn't last through a whole mass and decided to stay home, there was no play allowed with friends for the rest of that Sunday.

To us kids, our pastor Fr. McEntee was God Himself. It wasn't difficult for us to be in awe. He was well over six feet tall, and had snow-white hair and black teeth. He always dressed in shabby black greasy suits or in a long black clerical cassock as shiny as mom's crystal after being buffed up for the Christmas dinner. Fr. McEntee never had much money because he was always giving it away. I for one didn't mind getting up on a cold winters morning to serve, as I knew that I would receive a shiny sixpence or a shilling after I had extinguished the candles and carefully put my surplice and cassock back carefully in the altar boys' closet.

Because the rumor was that Fr. McEntee could cure people of various diseases and maladies, people came from far and near for a blessing from this saintly priest. Some were genuinely sick. Others were beggars who knew him as a soft touch who would quickly hand them any money he had. Next to my hero

Uncle Michael, Fr. McEntee had the most influence on my early decision to be a priest.

Fr. McEntee was also the manager of Legaginney National School, where seven of us Corr kids received our first formal education. The school was primitive, with only two classrooms for all nine grades. We entered the classrooms through sculleries, where our coats were hung in the winter and which also served to store the turf for the fires that were the only heat in the school even on the coldest of days. Master McCarthy, the principal and a trained teacher, taught grades five through eight.

Miss Bridget Gaffney, who had never attended college or training school, taught grades kindergarten through fourth grade. The most loved and respected person in the whole community, Miss Gaffney was a natural and multi-talented teacher who trained us well in all subjects, but especially in our penmanship and arithmetic. (Unfortunately, Miss Gaffney must be turning in her grave as she looks down from heaven at my poor penmanship today.) Most of all, Miss Gaffney nourished our childish faith with a deep reverence for Jesus, Son of God, His mother Mary and her husband Joseph. So well tutored by that saintly teacher Miss Gaffney, I still remember the emotion of being filled with the Holy Spirit when I received my First Holy Communion from Fr. McEntee.

All of our love and respect for saintly Fr. McEntee suddenly went out the window one Monday morning when, without warning, he walked into Miss Gaffney's room and tried to replace her with a trained teacher on the spot. When Miss Gaffney and all the kids began to cry, the saintly priest lost his cool and stomped out. Master McCarthy came rushing in, only to hear us screaming for the whole country to hear, "We want Miss Gaffney." We peeked through the crack in the door to the scullery where the master and the new teacher had gone to talk. When they returned, the master announced his solution of dividing the classes, but, alas, that solution lasted only for one week. Miss Gaffney was forced to transfer to another parish school eight miles away. We kids never forgave Fr. McEntee, especially since Miss Gaffney was found dead in her bed two years later. We were certain that she had died of a broken heart.

Outside of school, hunting was a favorite pastime for the Corr boys. P.Joe was an avid hunter and fisherman who would teach anyone willing to learn. When my older brothers went off to college, it was my turn to teach my two little brothers to fish and hunt. One day, out in the nearby Drumcarbin woods, we had five dogs - two small terriers trained to raise the rabbits out from the bushes and three fast greyhounds to catch them before they got away. On this particularly lucky day, instead of a little rabbit, there popped out what we later discovered was a beautiful silver fox.

Upon sighting the animal, the dogs bolted in pursuit. One of the strongest greyhounds grabbed the fox by the tail as it attempted to jump a wire fence. Soon the fox soon lay lifeless at our feet, leaving us the job of carrying the fox the four miles back to Legaginney House. That afternoon we paraded to town to sell the valuable fur. We embellished the story, certain that we Corr boys were the best hunters of all, as other groups had been pursuing this same fox in vain for several weeks with their better-trained hunting dogs and fancier rifles.

Back in the forties and fifties there wasn't any television in Ireland, and only a few families in the parish had radios. Children and teenagers had to create their own entertainment. As we reached seventh or eighth grade, we Corr boys were allowed to hang out with other boys at Lacken crossroads, forty yards up the road and a hundred yards down the hill from St.Michael's Church. Whenever I finished my duties at mass or a church event, I would rush to join the others at the crossroads to play pitch and toss or, better yet, skittles.

The skittle bets were small, only three pennies a game. The real fun was not so much on winning money as it was in winning the applause of the guys sitting on the fence across from Pat Lynch's shop. When the game was particularly good, the gang would gather round, yelling and encouraging their friends to make a big strike. Sometimes the cheering and screaming was so loud it could have been a bullfight in Spain or Mexico. In the summertime the bigger lads played handball down the road at the ball alley. The handball was serious business to the adults since it involved a league and competition with other parishes. We were the ball boys, dashing to recover balls hit over the back wall or smacked wildly over the railroad tracks.

It was daylight in Ireland until ten o'clock in the evening during the summer. As the games ended we would all, the boys and the men, congregate on the crossroads fence across from Pat Lynch's shop. Sometimes that was when the real fun began, as Irish wit came most alive whenever anyone started to tell a story. As kids we usually remained quiet unless we were asked a question by one of the adults. There were stories good and bad - about politics, Gaelic football, and about family members who had emigrated to America, Australia, and England to find work and send money to their families back home. Nobody told off-color jokes because Fr. McEntee, sitting on his porch twenty yards up the road, could easily overhear the conversation.

It is nearly dark now - time for us Corr boys to run home quickly to Legaginney House, past the school, past the Beattys', up the lane, and with no time to visit the McCuskers. To tell Mama Nell that we are late for the family rosary because Johnnie Moore was telling a great story is not an acceptable excuse. Mom leads the rosary, except when she is away visiting her sisters. Dad takes the first round of ten Hail Marys and an Our Father. It is a solemn, contemplative moment until our sister Dympna decides she is going to mimic an old lady from the top of Potahee Mountain and mumble the Hail Marys through her nose, sending all of us into a fit of giggling. Dad, upset at not knowing who or what is causing the laughter, puts an end to our giggling with a little sermon: "How do you all expect Jesus and His Mother to bless our home if we have no respect for them during the rosary?" We count ourselves lucky to make it to bed without a spanking. In the boys' room we recall the evening's fun at the crossroads as we fall asleep, together, in Legaginney.

Chapter 2

Nell and John Frank

As a child, I never felt as close to Dad as I did to Mom. Our dad John Frank was a man of his time who believed that, for his sons, hard outdoor work made the man. His education ended after seventh grade. His only weaknesses were smoking cigarettes and having a quick Irish temper that he passed on to most of us kids, including me. He never drank alcohol, which was unusual for an Irish man. He loved farming and eagerly awaited the arrival of each springtime to begin plowing and planting.

Farming in Ireland in the forties and fifties was tough. As a little boy I always watched with eagerness as, perched high on the mowing machine, Dad began cutting the corn. He always began his work, whether it was harvesting corn or digging a field of potatoes, with, "Let's start, lads, in the name of God." Dad was committed to the farm and expected each of his six sons to be the same as soon as we came of age. I was a hard worker, and he liked that. But he didn't realize that I worked hard only so that I could finish sooner and be free to swim or play at Lacken crossroads. When he bought a second farm on a beautiful lake six miles away, he may have thought, "This one is for Finbarr."

Nell, our mom, had different ideas. A college graduate who believed strongly in education, she held the priesthood in the highest regard. Nothing would have pleased her more than if all six of her sons had entered the seminary. Perhaps because of Mom's influence, I loved serving mass and participating in all the liturgical practices in church like Benediction of the Blessed Sacrament and the Stations of the Cross. Under her guidance, when I was only eight I demonstrated my personal devotion to the Blessed Virgin Mary by saying the rosary every day for a month. I was especially close to Mom during my preteen years. I helped her feed the chickens, ducks, and geese, her "fund-raisers" for our boarding school tuitions and also for the weekly rations of tea, bread, and butter for the family. Mom's egg money was frequently the target of our pleadings when we wanted some easy cash for going to town or to a parish dance.

We knew that Mom was a much easier touch than Dad. The story in the family was that, as a young boy, Dad asked his own parents for money to go to the County Fair in Cavan. They gave him a sixpenny piece and told him to have a good time. Dad continued the tradition of stinginess when it came to giving us pocket money. If one of us asked him for two shillings to go a dance or football game, he gave two shillings and nothing more. He wouldn't think of adding a few pennies for a soda or sweets.

Somehow we never felt negatively toward him. We realized that he worked hard and depended mostly upon the monthly checks from the creamery for the milk he sold them daily. His only other major source of income was from selling two-year-old calves at the local fair. Jack Murtagh, my oldest brother P.Joe, and Dad would walk the herd the five miles to the fair in Cavan town. The price that day determined the mood in which he came home that evening.

Even when times were bad, Dad and Mom were generous with their donations to the Church and to various charities. From an early age, we Corr kids were reminded of our responsibilities - that God had given us personal gifts and treasures and we in turn should share with the needy in our community and with the poor throughout the world. Our home, like many others, had its own mite box. Mom had a special place in her heart for the tinkers who came to our home to sell tin cans or buckets. In addition to feeding them, she would give them our hand-me-down clothes and discuss whether their children had made their First Holy Communion.

From Mom I learned how to reach out spiritually to others. From Dad I learned how to exercise my civic responsibility. A veteran of the Irish Republican Army (IRA), the group that resisted the English occupation of Ireland, Dad continued his political mission by serving as a member of the county council. Unlike most Irish politicians, Dad was very humble and didn't brag about his achievements. On election days, proud of him, we were always eager to help in whatever ways children could. P.Joe would transport older neighbors to the election booth on the horse and trap.

Once some of the local farmers offered to vote a second time for Dad by using the name of a recently deceased parishioner. Dad wouldn't consider it. "If I am not elected fair and square, I don't want any part of it," he'd say. All of us had reason to celebrate the next morning when it was announced that John Francis Corr had topped the poll by getting the most votes of all the candidates in the county.

Before we had a car, Dad would ride six miles on his bicycle into Cavan town for the monthly county council meetings. Local people often sought his support in helping them get civil service jobs in the county. Without any hesitation he would mount his bike and ride with the candidate to visit other council members and recruit their support. All of this was done without pay or gratuity. He would share stories of people he had met and how he had influenced other council members to change their vote on a project.

Part of Dad's responsibility as a councilman was to serve on the board of the local mental hospital in County Monaghan. He had great sympathy for the mental patients and wanted us to understand that mental illness was serious and not a laughing matter. Dad met patients who thought they were Jesus Christ or the emperor of Japan. He would always end these stories with an admonition of how we should thank God for the blessing of having good mental health. He admonished us to have respect for all, especially the mentally ill.

With Mom's encouragement, I worked hard in school and got good grades. I was tired of cleaning cowsheds and picking potatoes on cold evenings, and soon came to the conclusion that a good education would be my ticket out of all the drudgery. I spent hours studying in my room with the belief that one day I would go over the hill at the top of the farm and never return.

My desire to become a priest like Fr. Michael was still very strong, but my desire to spend time with girls became stronger as I reached puberty. Unfortunately, sex education was not on the agenda at Legaginney National School. The only "formal education" about sex was when a visiting priest condemned adulterers and fornicators at a parish mission. Since our parents didn't talk to us about sex, we were left to figure it out for ourselves. One of my classmates had learned in confession that masturbation was a mortal sin. Upon receipt of this knowledge we excluded this activity so as not to spend all eternity in hell. I was very conflicted. I would have no problem deciding to become a priest if it included having a wife and sexual relations, but this was not the Church's way. A priest was to be married to his ministry and could not have time for a wife and children.

The subtle message I heard was that even though sex is pleasurable, it is bad, dirty, and only permissible if a couple engage in it to have children. As altar boys, we had assisted the pastor as he purified or "churched" women after they had babies. The not-so-subtle message was that, because the woman had given birth, she must have had sex with her husband and thus needed cleansing to be accepted back into the Church.

Being a good Catholic boy, I prayed for purity and decided early on that, in order to get to heaven and avoid all those sexual sins, I should follow the path I had intended for myself since early childhood. By the age of thirteen I decided that, for better or worse, I would choose chastity and celibacy. I looked to God and believed that, if He wanted me to be a priest, He would give me the strength and grace to persevere in chastity.

Master McCarthy encouraged Mom to send me to St. Patrick's College in Cavan, which two of my older brothers had also attended. There were some serious obstacles. Dad was disappointed that I didn't want to be a farmer and also had very little money left to pay tuition at St. Pat's after putting four of my siblings through boarding school. Determined, I was forced to face Dad and pose the question: "How can I become a student at St Pat's?" To my surprise, Dad, who had once called me muttonhead in a fit of anger when I wasn't concentrating on the job at hand, patiently said, "Why do you want to attend college?" When I nervously explained my reason, he felt very bad and answered ever so slowly, "Son, I don't have the money, but if you have this desire, I am sure Mom and I will find a way."

As usual, Mom came up with a plan of action to which Dad gave his passive assent. I would solicit help from Dad's brother Fr. Larry, who lived seventeen miles away in Cootehill. In 1949 we didn't have a home telephone, so one sunny morning I jumped on my bicycle and set off on my mission.

Fr. Larry, very surprised and happy to see me, complimented me on my courage for riding seventeen miles to visit him. He was a fun uncle, but I knew that asking him for money would turn a fun uncle into a quite cantankerous one. I let him tease me and chat about football before I presented my petition to him. "Father Larry," I explained, "I am desperate. I need your financial help to go to St. Patrick's College." He replied, half in anger, "Your parents are not good money managers, are they?" Even though I was tempted to jump on my bicycle and ride away, I ignored his attack on my parents and said, "Uncle, I want to be a priest just like you and Fr. Michael." His mood changed immediately. "Okay," he said, "go ahead. I will call the college to tell them you are coming." I thanked him profusely and headed home a very happy fellow.

Once again, Mom had proven to be very smart. She always seemed to say and do the right thing at the right time. Once when I was only twelve, an older boy beat me up in school. I came home in tears, very depressed, saying to Mom, "I cannot even defend myself." She grabbed me, hugged me close to her breast, and said reassuringly, "Finbarr, don't worry about it. I believe you are a wonderful young man and one day you are going to do something very special with your life."

When we kids were restless on a long winter's evening, Mom would push back the large kitchen table and pull out her violin or accordion. Only the girls in our family were allowed to take dancing lessons from a professional teacher. Even though Dad was a pretty good dancer himself, he forbade the boys to take lessons because he was afraid of our becoming sissies. That didn't stop me, who loved to dance, from secretly learning a few steps when my sister Dympna practiced what she was learning from the teacher.

My mom was one of the most attractive women I have ever met. Tommy Baxter, the local shoemaker, told us Corr kids that he and many of the local guys had been very jealous of my dad when he brought home his beautiful bride from County Longford. Tommy would add an accolade of his own, saying, "Your mother is the most beautiful woman that ever walked up the Main Street of Ballinagh."

We all loved to tease Mom about it. Embarrassed, she would reply, "Look at me now after ten pregnancies." She had gained a few pounds, but it was all proportionately distributed. She always walked with a particularly light gait for a big woman. When we pressed her to talk about how she and Dad had met and what their courtship had been like, she would reluctantly tell us that she was introduced to Dad at a house dance at the home of his cousins. During the courtship, he would travel the thirteen miles each Sunday morning in a beautiful trap drawn by a very handsome mare named Maggie. He would take Mom to mass in the local church two miles away, have dinner with her family, and then have Maggie trot him back to Legaginney. We would tease Mom further by asking, "Did this end your teaching career?" She would have the right answer as usual: "God had other plans for me, raising and teaching all of you."

Dad was chauvinistic but he would never admit it. Even as a twelve-year-old I knew that Dad was often wrong, but I also realized that Mom, being the smarter of the two, learned to dance around Dad rather than try to change his old habits. Once, all the men sat at the kitchen table while Mom struggled to get dinner on the table. She asked gently, "Would one of you boys please put the potatoes on the table?" Dad interrupted her immediately, and said, "I am sorry, Mam, my boys are to work in the fields and won't be sissies in the kitchen."

Knowing that Mom was hurt and embarrassed, I took a chance and said, "I don't mind being a sissy for a minute," and I put the potatoes on the table. Dad was irritated, but I knew he would get over it. Whether she ever challenged him when they were alone, I don't know. She certainly never chose to challenge him before her boys. Even though Dad had a quick temper, I don't remember him ever losing it with Mom.

Dad really lost his temper with me once. Jack Murtagh, P.Joe, Colm, and I had worked hard in the field all day. The hay was now ready to be pushed into big heaps and made into cocks. Since it was now six o'clock, our usual time to stop, and since the weather forecast for the next day was good, we saw no need to give up our football game to finish the project. Dad had been away that day at one of his council meetings and arrived in the hayfield just as we were ready to unhitch our horse and head off. Without as much as saying "Good job, boys" or asking if we were willing to work later than usual to finish the job, he presumed that we would continue.

My quick temper got the better of me. I ran over to him and protested. This was the first time I had ever confronted him. If he hadn't been sitting high on the wheel rake, I am sure I would have received a blow on the side of my head. Instead, he muttered to the horse to get moving, and we didn't leave the hayfield until ten P.M., certainly too late for any football. Dad told Mom later that night how utterly disappointed he was in me and how I needed to learn to respect him and all elders.

I loved my dad and, from my early childhood, yearned for his approval. No doubt, Dad probably thought that if he praised me I would have gotten a bigger head, which he seemed to think was big enough already! I learned only indirectly that he was proud of me. One day the postman shouted from the road to where I was working in the field, "Finbarr, your mom said to tell you that you passed your Intermediate Exam with five honors." Ecstatic, I jumped off the wheel rake and ran over to tell Dad. "Daddy, Daddy," I shouted, "I passed my exams with five honors!" His only reply was, "Good, keep the horse moving before he gets cold." I was crestfallen. The next day the herdswoman who tended our cattle congratulated me for doing so well on my exam. When I asked how she had heard, she smiled and replied, "Your dad told me, he is so proud."

Christmas with Nell and John Frank was always special. Uncles, aunts, cousins, and neighbors would stop in without warning for a cup of tea and a piece of Mom's Christmas pudding. Although neither Mom nor Dad was a regular drinker, Dad would offer the men a brandy or a glass of scotch. Once a year, on Christmas day, Mom would take a glass of port wine. We could see that she didn't like the idea of drinking alcohol at all. As adults we later commented that she looked so guilty drinking the wine that a person would think she had committed adultery. Under our parents' influence, each and every Corr kid took the pledge at Confirmation not to drink alcohol until we were twenty-five years old, and several pledged to abstain for life.

Growing up under the guidance of our caring, religious mother and hard-working father gave us values and a stability that we could always rely on wherever life took us. I was grateful for what my parents taught me, and never minded that there were eight other children who also required their attention and with whom I had to share. There were many advantages. My sister Eilish, a beauty like Mom, and the Carnival Queen at Stradone, spoiled me with candy and toys. Marie was a natural teacher who supervised our learning at home and forbade us to go to school with sloppy homework. Dympna liked to clean house, and tidied our rooms so well that none of us could find our clothes afterwards.

Most importantly, some of the nagging restrictions imposed during our childhood were subsequently overcome: my love of dancing survived and thrived, and, most baffling of all, even though we boys were denied culinary education, five of us somehow turned out to be good cooks.

Chapter 3

St. Pat's Cavan

As the day for eighth-grade graduation from Legaginney National School approached, the only students remaining in my class were Sean Mulligan, my cousin Nuala Phillips, and I. As was often the case in Ireland at that time, most of the class had already departed to help farm or to apprentice. We three sat in the last row of Master McCarthy's room. Since we had already passed all our important tests, the master left us alone. Sean and I talked about girls, sex, and football.

I couldn't tell Sean and Nuala that I had plans to become a priest. I had already told them that I had a serious crush on Patty Brady, a classmate in seventh grade. I would sneak up to Patty's seat and put a toffee sweet on her desk when Master McCarthy was busy correcting the homework. When Patty gave a quick look, I always winked, which caused her to turn beet red. I don't know what I would have done if she had responded more positively. To me, she was a gorgeous young lady with beautiful curly hair, buxom breasts, and a contagious smile. I wondered what it would be like to kiss her, with her two front teeth protruding a little beyond her lower lip. .

Because there weren't enough desks for all the fifth-grade students, many of them had to sit on long wooden stools along the wall to the left of where Sean, Nuala, and I sat. When Master McCarthy wasn't looking, Sean and I would tease the fifth graders, especially the girls. One day, the teasing went too far. Wanting to know the color of each girl's knickers, or panties, I secretly stretched a string from the leg of one fifth grader's stool across to our desk and tied it about one foot above the floor. When Master McCarthy dismissed everybody for lunch, our plan was that the girls would make their usual rush for the exit, trip over the string, and fall over each other, thus displaying their underwear. The prank worked perfectly. The first two girls tripped and the next two then fell head over heels on top of them. Sean and I laughed hysterically. Nuala didn't think it was so funny and was delighted when Master McCarthy discovered that the girls' tumble was not an accident. I quickly decided to throw myself at the mercy of the master.

He glared at me and said, "Finbarr Corr, if I expel you now, the possibility of your going to St. Patrick's College is out the window." Appropriately frightened that with one foolish act I had completely destroyed my future, I apologized profusely and promised to be on my best behavior for the rest of the term. I was very grateful that none of my sisters was still at the school, as they would have delighted in rushing home to tell my parents of the incident. Fortunately, Patty Brady was impressed by my honesty.

June 26th, 1949, our last day at Legaginney School, came too soon. I wanted to stay forever. I was sad that I wouldn't be seeing Patty Brady any more except in church. Now there would be no way that I could go up to her pew and give her toffee, and kissing her would forever be only a fantasy. I spent the early part of that summer working with Jack Murtagh and P.Joe in the bog. Later in the summer, I farmed with Dad and spent my spare time playing football with my friends. The summer went all too quickly, and soon it was time to pack.

Mom was a proud woman and didn't want her son to attend college poorly dressed. She had saved a few pounds by selling the extra eggs, chickens, and turkeys not needed for our own consumption. On the Tuesday before I was scheduled to leave, Mom and I boarded the bus at Miss Berrill's railroad crossing and headed for Mom's favorite shop, Philip McDonald's on Main Street in Cavan. Because Mrs. McDonald was one of Mom's confidants, Mom could tell her that our finances were not flush, and she would give Mom a break.

Mrs. McDonald's son Leo took me over to the boys' section and dressed me in long blue pants, a white shirt with a blue-and-yellow tie, and a blue sweater. Along with the college-peaked cap, this was the required dress uniform for our parades from the college into Cavan town to attend special services at the Cathedral of St. Felim. Mom smiled when I returned from the dressing room in my new clothes, but I could see a little tear in the corner of her eye. Mom whispered to her dear friend, "He wants to be a priest." Mrs. McDonald promised to pray for me.

On Tuesday morning, dressed in my new uniform, I started up the lane to say goodbye to Bridget and Phildy McCusker. This time Mrs. McCusker shoved two half crowns in my pocket, and this time Phildy was watching. When I protested at such a great sum, Phildy surprised me, saying, "We are both proud of you. We want you to have some money when the priests take you to football games in town."

It was always hard to say goodbye to old Mrs. Beatty and her husband Jimmy. After giving me two shillings, Mrs. Beatty hugged me and said, "Son, I hope I am here when you come home at Christmas. When you get to my age, you never know when God is going to call you home."

My godfather Frank Corr gave me a few more shillings. With fourteen shillings in my pocket, I felt rich. When I told Dad about my good fortune, he asked if I was going to take it all to college, or leave it with him as my savings. Mom intervened and said, "Let him take it all. I surely don't want him to be embarrassed when his classmates are buying sweets and fruits on their days off."

After an early lunch, Dad hitched our favorite mare, Maggie, into the trap. Mom had neatly packed all my bedclothes, an extra pair of corduroy pants, pajamas, socks, my football boots, toothbrushes, and other belongings in a large wooden trunk. Dad loaded the trunk into the trap, which left just enough room for him and me but none for Mom. With tears flowing down her cheeks, she hugged me goodbye. I cried quietly. I didn't want Dad to call me a sissy.

At Dad's command, Maggie trotted down the narrow lane and onto the Legaginney Road. We stopped at Miss Berrill's to let the one o'clock train go through on its way from Crossdoney to Dublin. Dad didn't say much during the one-hour drive. I was afraid to ask him whether he was disappointed that I was not staying home to be a farmer like him. I remembered a statement that Master McCarthy had taught us: "Let a sleeping dog lie."

Dad finally broke the silence just as we were entering the college gates. He announced, "We have a surprise for you. Your cousin Brian Corr is also starting today. His mom and dad have arranged that you two will be roommates." I was thrilled. Brian was a year younger than I, but was one class ahead because he had attended the reputable Christian Brothers School in Cavan town.

Brian and his parents entered our room at about the same time as Dad and I did. Brian unpacked his trunk and put his clothes in the drawers with very little help from his mom. I followed suit and then proceeded to try to make my bed. Seeing the result, Aunt Maura exclaimed, "Oh, Finbarr, that won't do. It looks like a pig's bed in Legaginney."

I wanted to reply, "Aunt Maura, my dad would not allow us to make our own beds because he didn't want us to grow up sissies like your two boys." But instead I said simply, "Thanks for your help, Aunt Maura." Brian's father, Uncle Barney, was more empathetic. He pulled me outside the bedroom to tell me not to worry, that he hadn't known how to make a bed either when he had come to St. Pat's as a student forty years ago but somehow had managed to go on to both a successful career and a successful life.

This was to be the first of many embarrassments, that I, the boy from the country, would experience living with the more sophisticated boys from the towns. For the next year, I would frequently hear our science professor John McBreen say, "You can take the man from the bog, but you cannot take the bog from the man."

It was the custom at St. Pat's from time immemorial that the second-year students had the right to initiate the freshmen boys. Because I was from the country and not a robust kid, I was one of the first to be "baptized." Two burly second year guys grabbed me by both arms while a third guided me into the bathroom. They asked me what nickname I would like to have. Being a little naïve, I said, "My oldest brother P.Joe was called Dead Cow, and my next brother Jack was The Calf." I got off easy. They held my head under the coldwater tap. The third student turned on the water and recited, "We hereby give you the name of Little Calf." Later I discovered that the priest faculty and the senior school prefects knew of the ritual and gave tacit assent as long as there wasn't any brutality. Because my cousin Brian and my new friends the Scott brothers were townies, I was more protected than any of the other country boys.

We started classes immediately, and it quickly became obvious why Professor Breen reached out to help the country boys. We were academically far behind the town boys, who were already quite proficient in algebra and geometry. I was determined to catch up with the townies by the time of the first house exam before the Christmas holidays. When other students were asleep at 10 P.M., and all the bedroom lights had been turned off by the master switch, I would sneak out to a light in the corridor to study my geometry for another hour. At Christmas I passed the geometry exam by nine points.

I enjoyed the liturgies at the college and kept myself motivated by thinking that one day I would be up there as celebrant of the mass. Each Sunday we were required to attend two masses. While most of the boys resented it, I used the opportunity to fantasize about myself as a priest - raising the host, raising the chalice, and saying "Corpus Christi (Body of Christ)" as I gave out communion. I volunteered to serve mass as often as I could.

I also helped the student sacristan, whose nickname was Holy John. Once while I was carrying the largest crucifix for the Stations of the Cross, I slipped on the marble in sanctuary and fell on top of the crucifix, bending it in the middle. While I was still sprawled on the floor, Holy John decided that the show must go on. He stepped over me, took up the bent crucifix, and continued the procession to the first Station. All the students were laughing hysterically. The college dean, who was presiding, joined in the laughter but finally called for reverence as he helped me, embarrassed but not injured, to my feet. When I opened my missal the next morning, some wise guy had written, "The First Station, Finbarr falls underneath his cross."

Every year we had a five-day retreat. During this period, all of us were expected to observe absolute silence except when answering the responses at mass or confessing our sexual sins to the retreat master. The latter was a very difficult task for a fourteen-year-old boy from the country, especially one whose only sexual experience was fantasizing about kissing Patty Brady.

The retreat master usually didn't pull any punches. He stared down at all of us and said, "Masturbation is a very grave sin. It is mortal, punishable in hell for all eternity." As if this wasn't enough to put the fear of God in all of us, he would further expand this sermon to say that the Blessed Virgin Mary would cry for an hour each time a boy masturbated. He also listed possible side effects for this heinous crime. Lowering his voice, he emphasized, "Masturbation is not good for your health. It is equivalent to losing a pint of blood, and continual masturbation will definitely affect your eyesight."

Another sin he mentioned was mugging, which I had never heard of. It seemed that it involved two people and, since ours was an all-boys school, I presumed it somehow involved two boys. When I asked my cousin Brian and the Scott brothers about this peculiar sin, they were of no help. I had to wait until the Christmas holidays when my brother P.Joe came to pick me up. With Maggie trotting us home to Legaginney, I waited until there was no traffic to distract P.Joe from what I feared would be a difficult conversation. P.Joe gave me an opening. He casually asked me, "Well, how do you like St. Pat's?"

I told him that I had to work very hard to catch up with the townies in algebra and geometry, but that I really enjoyed the new subjects of physics and chemistry. Then, with all the sensitivity I could muster, I asked him, "What is mugging?" He stuttered a little and said, "I should have warned you about that, and I hope you are not involved in it." He went on to say that it is a sexual act performed between senior boys and younger feminine-looking boys that serve as substitutes since no girls are available.

I still didn't understand it fully, but I expressed my thanks to P.Joe and reassured him I was not active in mugging. As I grew older, I realized that it was practiced in epidemic proportions in many of the boarding schools in Ireland, and according to rumor, two of our priest professors were reported to Bishop Quinn by some senior students who accused the professors of similar pedophile acts with junior boys.

My first year at St. Pat's was challenging. The second and third years were easier and happier. I made many good friends like Michael Smyth, a nephew of the Smyths who owned the well-known

Railway Hotel. We would skip into the hotel for extra food on our way to sports games in Breifne Park.

One of the real negatives of St. Pat's, and perhaps the only negative, was the poor food served in the dining room. We had porridge, tea, and toast for breakfast. Occasionally, we had fried eggs, or should I say "rock" eggs. The nearly inedible eggs were usually so overcooked by the time they were served that they could have been used for skittles back at Lacken crossroads.

To compensate for this poor food, we came up with many ingenious ways to supplement our diets. A few of us who were braver honed our skill in raiding Bishop Quinn's orchard next door to the college. We would usually plan our trip on nights when there was a full moon. Two or three of us would get our large laundry bags and, at 1 A.M. when we were reasonably certain that the bishop and our own college priests were fast asleep, we would sneak past the ball alley and football field and shimmy over the wire fence that protected the orchard. Once inside, one of us climbed the apple and pear trees by the light of the moon and tossed fruit to our two buddies below until we had filled three bags. Back in our bedrooms, we stowed the fruit in our trunks, hidden under our beds.

Our only big scare was when the bishop's dog came into the orchard while two of us were already up in two trees. I took a chance of trying to befriend the dog by whistling and pretending to know him. He stopped barking and approached to let me pat his head. The following day, I suggested to my two fellow thieves that we should call Bishop Quinn and tell him that his dog, while possibly useful for hunting pheasants and wild ducks, wasn't worth a damn as a watchdog.

Having escaped without being bitten by the dog or caught by the bishop or his housekeepers, we decided to dare another way of creating "feeds." Since the lift down to the kitchen was just ten feet away from our bedroom, we decided to switch our focus from the bishop's orchard to the college kitchen as the object of our mission. There was only one snag. Once we reached the kitchen, we found everything locked.

I knew that my cousin Pat Phillips, a senior prefect, kept the master key to all locks in the college in his pants pocket, so I volunteered to sneak into his bedroom when he was sleeping and borrow the keys for a couple of hours. The task was easier than I thought. Without needing to use my flashlight, I could see Pat's pants hanging over the end of the iron bed. I was as quiet as a church mouse as I took his keys without as much as moving a leg of his pants.

Within ten minutes we had opened the locked doors in the kitchen and loaded up our laundry bags with fancy breads usually saved for the priests and their guests. We also took eggs, canned goods, and other treats and were back upstairs in twenty minutes. Armed with the powerful master key, we then took the eggs down to the science lab and cooked them on Bunsen burners. What a feast in the middle of the night!

Two weeks later, when I begged off the expedition because of flu, my colleagues were outwitted by Fr. Charles Travers, a science professor and volunteer part-time detective determined to catch the thieves. His method was simple and creative. He placed purple dye on the knobs of the kitchen door. When my colleagues touched the knob, the dye stuck to their hands. No big deal, right? Not so. When the thieves returned to their rooms and washed their hands in the enamel basins, the dye remained on the surface and would not wash away. All that the dean needed to do was to make his rounds of the rooms the next morning to discover which basins were stained with the purple dye. Even though I had loaned a torch to the thieves, my basin was clean and I escaped indictment once again.

For all practical purposes, I remained sexually illiterate during my years at St. Pat's. The message from retreats and confessors was that a sexual sin was always grave and that it was a mortal sin merely to entertain thoughts of doing sexual acts. Yet I was fascinated by human sexuality and wondered from an early age that if God created us male and female, He must also have created sexual feelings and implanted in men and women a desire for the physical union with each other. Like all young Irish boys, I talked a lot about sex and told a lot of sexual jokes, yet remained a virtual virgin through my five years of boarding school.

One final Easter vacation, May Daly, an older neighbor, introduced me to a young lady friend of hers in town named Dympna. As they would say back then, Mary Daly was "playing gooseberry" for Dympna and Finbarr. The relationship was largely platonic, and our only activity was long walks through Tuberrora Lane, a traditional lovers' hangout. We had just two dates, the second one ending with a couple of passionate kisses and touches outside the clothes that didn't even seem grave enough even to mention in confession.

When I returned to St. Pat's for the final six weeks, everyone was sharing his post-graduation plans.

Whenever people asked me what I planned on doing after St. Pat's, I would simply say with a straight face, "I plan to join the Palestine Police in Israel." Because I had always been a fun-loving guy who played pranks on fellow students and professors alike, I shocked my classmates when I finally announced my plan to follow my three uncles and older brother Jack into the priesthood. When the powers-that-be in the college heard about my desires, they immediately attempted to recruit me for the home diocese of Kilmore. At that time, vocations to the priesthood were so popular in Ireland that only the brightest students were accepted for the Irish parishes. But, intent on going to America, I resisted the offer.

When I passed my Leaving Certificate exam in June, I had already been admitted as a seminarian at another St. Patrick's College, this one in the town of Carlow, forty miles south of Dublin. With some help from my brother Jack, I applied and was accepted as a candidate in the priesthood for the diocese of Paterson, New Jersey. Bishop James A. McNulty of Paterson wrote me a very warm welcoming letter with the news that the diocese would pick my tuition tab at St. Patrick's Carlow.

In the meantime, the news of my intention to enter the priesthood must have reached Ballinagh where Dympna lived. When I came home in June and picked her up to go to the movies as usual, she said, "What's this I hear – you are going to be a priest? Why are you continuing to see me?" I replied very sheepishly, "Dympna, I am very fond of you and we are not doing anything wrong." Unfortunately, that was our last date.

My colleagues from Legaginney with whom I played Irish football and hung out at parish dances hadn't a clue about my plans after I graduated from St. Pat's in Cavan. That summer I tagged along to dances and carnivals and particularly enjoyed the deception of not telling them that I was entering the seminary in September and that my days of chasing girls would soon come to a screeching halt. That summer would be, in the words of the famous Irish-American writer Edwin O'Connor, my "last hurrah."

At one parish dance in Legaginney's hall, I invited a new girl out to do a quick step. We flew around the floor, her dress at full sail. As we ended the dance she wanted to keep dancing, as did I since she was an excellent partner. My friends teased, "Are you going for a walk to the parish house tonight?" I then learned that it was Fr. McGauran's new housekeeper whom I was brazenly swinging around the dance floor, which explained Father's intense stare at me from across the room.

In late August Barney Brady asked me, "Do you want a ride to the dance over in Gowna on Sunday night?" I smiled back and said, "I'd love to, Barney, but I'm off to the seminary tomorrow." He was in total shock and said, "Finbarr, it will be awful if you are ever ordained a priest." We both laughed and walked away.

Chapter 4

The Seminary

I was very excited when Pat Scott, my friend at St. Pat's in Cavan, also applied to the diocese of Paterson and was accepted. On September 4th, 1954, I said my goodbyes to the McCuskers and to old Mrs. Beatty. Pat's dad picked me up and drove us both, Pat and me, dressed in black suits and ties, the 110 miles to St. Patrick's Carlow. As we passed through the iron gates and up the driveway to the imposing four-story building, I felt the pressure to leave all thoughts of girls and sex outside those hallowed walls.

Fr. Kinsella, the junior dean, approached us. Dressed in his long black cassock, he said in an official voice, "Welcome to St. Patrick's Carlow. You can leave your luggage inside the door. We will call you all to the refectory in a little while." Without waiting for a reply or asking our names, he turned on his heels as if he were on automatic pilot and walked away. I ran over to Mr. Scott's car, and only half jokingly said, "You had better hold on for a few minutes. I'm not sure if Pat and I want to stay!"

Two new students from County Clare had arrived earlier in the day and had already unpacked. They were playing handball on one of the courts across from the football field. They introduced themselves: "I'm Des Fitzgerald and this is Mike Hayes." Feeling slightly depressed and lonesome, I took a rain check on an invitation from them to join their game. Little did I know then that this was the beginning of a friendship with Mike Hayes that would last for forty-six years.

After supper in the refectory, Fr. Kinsella addressed everyone. He read the dormitory assignments for the late arrivals, gave a brief welcome, and announced, "You fellows may as well get used to it. There will be solemn silence after supper until breakfast tomorrow morning." Now I really felt as though I was in Mountjoy, one of the toughest prisons in Ireland.

My new best friend Mike Hayes was in the cubicle to the right of me in the dormitory. Des Fitzgerald was to the right. There was a little hole in the wooden partition between Des and me. Before we went to sleep, Des broke the solemn silence as he whispered through the hole, "Goodnight, Finbarr. Don't let the bed-bug bite you." It felt good. I said, "Sleep tight, Des." Dan Kelleher, a very quiet chap from County Cork, slept on the other side of Des. We knew from the outset that Dan wouldn't break solemn silence even if the whole college was on fire.

Fr. Kinsella read more rules of the seminary the following morning. The twenty minutes of silence after the formal morning prayer was time for mental prayer, which Fr. Tom Brophy, the spiritual director of the seminary, would teach us. When the rising bell rang at 6 A.M., the challenge was to shower and shave, run fifty yards down a long corridor, and be in the chapel for morning prayer thirty minutes later. A few days later, I complained at breakfast to our Deacon Jim Feenan, the prefect in charge, that I always got a bad headache whenever I got out of bed suddenly that early in the morning. He nearly fell off his chair with laughter. He said that we would learn early on to "suck it up," as all the discipline was necessary to toughen us up for many challenging years in the priesthood.

Dan Kelleher became a model for Des Fitzgerald and me. Between classes Dan would visit the chapel to pray to Jesus in the tabernacle, and he was absolutely scrupulous about observing all the rules in the seminary. Didn't we receive a shock four weeks later when we found Dan packing his trunk to leave the seminary for good! Des and I asked him what was wrong. He said very solemnly, "I am not good enough to be a priest."

Fitz and I weren't worth tuppence the whole day. We figured that if Dan couldn't make it, what chance did we, recovering reprobates, have. Later that night, Fitz whispered through the little hole. "They are beginning to leave from the other end. You and I will be the last to leave." I nodded and laughed myself to sleep.

Our class of forty students was known as the First Philosophers. Early in the first term, all of us were due to be interviewed by Fr. "Holy Tom" Brophy, the spiritual director of the seminary. I was very honest with Holy Tom from the beginning, and confided that the only problem I worried about was sexuality and celibacy. I shared with him my limited sexual experience with Dympna, and how I avoided the mugging in boarding school. I asked him why masturbation was so bad since it didn't involve any other person. He opened the Bible and pointed out to me that people who do such things would not enter the kingdom of heaven. In a rueful and prophetic tone, he added, "God help you, Finbarr – going to America with all your good looks."

To help me learn to control my temper, Holy Tom instructed me that when kneeling and sitting in choir for daily mass, midday prayer, and night prayer, I should resolve not to look across the chapel to the seminarians sitting opposite me for a six-month period. It seemed impossible to me, who was always curious. I was often tempted, particularly when any person reading morning prayer mispronounced a saint's name and set everybody to giggling, but I still kept my head down. To my surprise, I was successful in my resolution. I have often asked myself since, "Why didn't Holy Tom have an exercise to help us comfortably control our sexual desires?"

My transition to the seminary was easier than my transfer from Legaginney School to St. Patrick's Cavan. By age nineteen, my self-esteem had improved, and my sense of humor helped me make friends easily. Although my family in Cavan was too far away to visit me regularly, my sister Eilish came at least once a semester to visit Pat Scott and myself. I was fortunate that a family named Shanaghy had moved to Carlow from our home parish in Potahee. Since I was not allowed to visit them, the Shanaghys came once a month with all kinds of goodies from their food shop, which helped us survive the poor food in the seminary.

The studies at Carlow were easy. I had developed good study habits to catch up with the townies at Cavan. History and geography, subjects that I found boring in boarding school, weren't required. The study of philosophy and logic fascinated me and laid a good foundation for the four years of theology that followed. Because of my hard work and competitive spirit, I was close to the top of the class, but I could never beat Mike Hayes. Mike easily seemed to absorb the most difficult of concepts and to remember what all the ancient fathers said about any subject. Fortunately, the student who had the highest mark didn't always receive the annual prize, which was drawn by lot among the top three scores in each subject area. The professor who read out the winners did so in Latin to add to the mystique. Whenever my name was drawn, the prize came with the announcement "Finbarr Corr *tulit*." To this very day, I don't know what the translation of *tulit* is. When the announcement was made, I would pump my fist towards Mike and walk up for my prize, often a big philosophical book that I would never read.

Except for visits to a local doctor or dentist, we were not allowed outside the college. There was one exception. In good weather the whole student body, dressed in their black suits and hats and carrying walking sticks, would go for a five- or six-mile walk once a week outside the town. This exercise was totally boring to me. It reminded me of a scene in a movie of prisoners shackled together going out to work on a highway.

As often was the case, I found a way to avoid what I disliked. A call went out for volunteers to help plant new shrubs around the seminary grounds. Since the planting activity was at the same time as the walks, I was among the first to volunteer. This time my country background was an advantage. When spring arrived and our work bloomed, we received many compliments - and teasing as well. Some classmates suggested perhaps we were choosing the wrong careers and that maybe we should go to a horticultural college. I was ready for their teasing, and said, "Don't you think Jesus was a pretty good carpenter before he started his public preaching at age thirty."

The one disadvantage in not going out on the Wednesday walks was that we didn't see any girls at all. When it came time for the bus trip home at Christmas, I was strangely afraid of both buses and girls because I had not seen either in four months.

We were expected to continue our prayer habits and attend daily mass while at home on vacations. That was the least of my worries. I was afraid of seeing Patty Brady at Potahee mass. I wondered if she would recognize that inside my black suit and tie was a very passionate young man who was struggling to repress all sexual feelings towards her.

We were allowed to attend house dances, but we were forbidden to go to church dances and definitely not to carnivals. From now on these would be considered occasions of sin. I missed dancing as a recreation. I had discovered in my teenage years that, like football and swimming, it was a great way to release tension. The girls with whom I danced, however, didn't see it that way. They would insist on dancing very close to me and occasionally one would whisper, "It is a shame you are going to be a priest. That is such a waste."

Once, when I was at a friend's wedding, the local pastor criticized one of the bridesmaids for dancing too close to me. He said, "Don't you realize that this young man is studying to be a priest? You are not supposed to dance that close to him." The same girl could have caused me real trouble if she had responded with the truth, that it was Finbarr who was holding her close. Mom was very empathetic and, like the pastor, blamed the girls more than me. She would say, "I know the girls find you attractive. Just be

41

careful or some of the neighbors could write a letter and report you to the president of the seminary."

Springtime in the seminary was uplifting. For me, the beauty of the trees and flowers reflected the beauty and power of God. I would often recall Mom's statement to me when I was only twelve: "You are a special young man, and you are going to do something special with your life." Deep down, I felt God calling me. I had faith enough to realize that if He could create such beautiful trees and flowers, He could also give me the grace to be a chaste priest.

By the third year, I had proven both to myself and to my professors that I had the intellectual and emotional capacity to be a fine priest. I could still make mistakes, such as pronouncing *Air Corps* as "Air Corpse" when I was the reader in the refectory. Unfortunately, our elocution professor and senior dean, Fr. Dowling, was monitoring lunch that day. He stopped at the podium as my classmates were giggling and said, "Mr. Corr, the word *Corps* has a French pronunciation." Humbled, I said, "Sorry, Father."

When we attained the level of First Theology that year, we moved from dormitories to rooms that housed two or three students. Some seminarians occupied an area we nicknamed Rotten Row, while others of us were located over the priest's refectory in a room nicknamed Sodom. I had two wonderful roommates - Michael McManus, a former classmate from Cavan, and my friend Mike Hayes. McManus and I were the talkative ones. Mike Hayes only talked when the topic was golf or drama. He never talked about sex or girls. He had no trouble keeping solemn silence. McManus and I decided that we would at least keep it for the penitential season of Lent, which started on Ash

Wednesday. What we didn't realize was that this attempt at penance for Lent would get both of us into serious trouble.

A rumor on our floor was that on Monday mornings there were always great cake and cookie leftovers on the table in the priests' dining room. One of the second-year theology students, known for his ability to escape being caught, was helping himself by raiding the dining room and treating himself and his roommates to all these delicacies. Very early one Monday morning, Michael McManus dressed quickly and left the room. Time passed, and he hadn't come back. Since we weren't talking, he hadn't told me where he was going.

I had separately planned a surprise for my two roommates that same morning. I would go down the stairs and sneak into the priest's dining room and, with the help of a lighted match, grab a few cakes and bring them back to our room for a feast during study period that evening. As usual, Mike Hayes was still in bed. My heart was thumping as I descended the stairs. The dining room door creaked a little as I opened it. As I groped for the table in the dark, I touched a head sitting at the table.

"Oh my God," I gasped. I thought I had touched a dead head. Actually, it belonged to Michael McManus, who was sitting in the dark at the table. Out of the dark, from the far side of the table, came a deep voice, "Sit down, mister." Frightened, I bolted out the door and down the corridor. The next thing I remember was standing alone at the first Station of the Cross in the senior chapel. It came as no surprise that I was soon joined in the chapel by Fr. Dowling, the man with the deep voice. With a funny grin on his face, he said, "I will see you and Mr. McManus in my office after breakfast."

To control the damage, Mike and I decided to keep the incident an absolute secret until after we received our punishment. We knew that Fr. Dowling wanted to gloat about his success as a would-be detective. If we told the story to any of his cronies, or kiss-up groupies as we called them, they would go to congratulate him. Our publicizing the event and the catch would then free Fr. Dowling to talk about it to everybody and leave us the laughing stock of the college. We hoped that we would only receive what for one hundred years had been called The Cat, short for "caveat."

At the appointed time we knocked on Fr. Dowling's living room door. His first comment was, "Have you guys packed your bags yet?" I figured it was a bluff. "Father," I said, "This is a first offense for both of us, and we realize we were out of bounds. I can say honestly for both of us that this was our first attempt at taking anything from the priest's dining room." We both received caveats, but this didn't affect our careers or our ultimate status in the seminary. We were not bestowed with the order of Lector that summer, but I was chosen as a prefect to supervise the diocesan boarding school, Knockbeg, the following spring.

Those of us who attended St. Patrick's Carlow all remember it as a seminary that served terrible food. Once, when the deacons walked out of the dining room in protest, the college hired a dietitian from Dublin to assess the situation. The chief cook knew that the dietitian was coming and prepared what she considered a most wonderful dinner. However, the dietician's judgment was still that even that special meal wasn't good enough for swine. One smart aleck said, "But it is good enough for seminarians."

The faculty at St. Pat's included Fr. Patrick Lennon, the president and also the school's only good scriptural scholar and expert on moral theology. When I sat for my orals during the final year, I discovered just how volatile Fr. Lennon was. He presented a problem to me in Latin that involved moral aspects of a pregnancy outside the womb, which can be life threatening to the mother. When I answered that the fetus should be removed to save the mother's life, he jumped from his desk, threw his cigarette in the fireplace, and said rather coldly, "So you would instruct the doctor to perform a direct abortion, Mr. Corr?" I had to think quickly. I said, "Father, I am sorry, I am very confident about my knowledge of moral theology, would you kindly repeat the question in English? I haven't been using Latin regularly for the past six years." I changed my answer and passed the test.

It is still difficult to forgive the faculty for letting us out on the missions to America while still so illiterate in human sexuality. The textbook on moral theology was mainly written in English. The two chapters dealing with the sixth and ninth commandments about adultery and desiring another man's wife were in Latin. When we asked the reason, the professors replied that they didn't want the publishing company's secretaries to know the details we were being taught about sex. The irony of it all was that the college secretary who assisted Fr. Lennon had taken four years of Latin in boarding school and commented that she enjoyed the material very much. The story was that whenever Fr. Lennon started teaching the chapters on sex, he turned off the classroom lights, pulled the shades down, lit blessed candles, and requested that all students place their hands on the desk during the lecture just in case, if sexually aroused by the discussion, they were tempted to play with themselves under the desk.

The appointment in March 1959 was one of the few really plum jobs in final year - prefect at the diocesan high school, St. Mary's Knockbeg. The prefects lived at the school, supervised the study halls, and saw that the students went to bed without killing each other in the dormitories. Each morning, the three deacon prefects would ride their bicycles four miles to the seminary and then return to Knockbeg in the afternoon. I loved the assignment and the freedom it brought. My friends the Shanaghys loved it also, as I could sneak into their store to do some shopping and have a good meal every so often. My classmates greatly appreciated my generosity and the risk I took in smuggling the Sunday papers in, since the rules otherwise restricted us to the weekly Catholic papers in the library.

All of my classmates were eagerly anticipating June 11th, 1960, our ordination day. In the weeks and months before, we had gone through the usual rituals – putting on a play for the rest of the student body, passing on whatever books we were not taking out to the missions with us, and drawing lots for the best seats in the cathedral for our families on ordination day. As usual, there was a lot of teasing and joking to hide any anxiety we might have had in taking that final and irrevocable step. In my mind, I kept repeating the Biblical phrase "You are a priest forever according to the order of Melchisedech." I felt confident, but I also had a healthy anxiety since I knew that celibacy could be a real challenge for me.

The final retreat was challenging and affirming. Holy Tom reviewed our journey and reflected how forty of us came to Carlow six years ago, and also how twenty four of us had reached our goal and would accept the greatest calling any man could receive – to become part of the priesthood of Jesus Christ. He told us not to be afraid, and reassured us that, as long as we stayed close to Jesus and his blessed mother in prayer, the grace of ordination would carry us over any hurdle. On the night before ordination, Fr. Dowling conducted one of the final rituals. He asked us to sign several forms signifying our willingness to accept ordination and obedience to the bishop of the diocese in which we were committed to serve.

Fr. Dowling had grown more relaxed with us as deacons and was a willing partner in teasing us and accepting our playful pranks. I felt comfortable enough on that evening to share with him that I was suffering from an embarrassing itch of the scrotum. With a straight face he said, "Why don't you go to Sister Josephine in the infirmary? I'm sure she has some lotions she could rub on it to relieve the itch." Then he broke into his customary belly laugh, letting all of my classmates know that something very funny happened.

To get back at him, I announced to all my classmates that if anybody had jock itch, Fr. Dowling had lotion and would apply it after we signed our commitments. My classmates agreed that I had won the battle of wits until Fr. Dowling added, "Finbarr has the itch where his vows are going to affect him the most."

The day of ordination neared, and my family began assembling. I was disappointed that my hero Fr.

47

Michael decided not to come from America. My brother Jack came and brought a fun-loving Irish-American priest named Jim Daly. Fr. Larry was there, proud as a peacock because he knew that without his support I might still be cleaning the cowsheds in Legaginney. Uncle Barney and Aunt Maura came early and pushed a beautiful gold watch over my left hand. Uncle Barney was in tears and gave me a big hug, saying, "Finbarr, we are so proud of you. You will be a great priest in America." Not surprisingly, my dad chose to stay home until the very last minute so that he could milk the cows early the next morning, so Fr. Gaffney from St. Michael's Potahee drove Mom and some of my siblings to Carlow.

The weather was absolutely beautiful on ordination day. All of my siblings, my parents, and my closest friends took their places in the Cathedral of the Assumption Carlow. By luck of the draw, my parents and some of my sisters and brothers were seated in the second row. It surely must have been a stirring sight to see twenty-four young men prostrated before old Bishop Keogh. When the bishop called us forth by name in Latin, each of us took a step forward and replied, "*Ad Sum* (I am ready)."

The bishop anointed my hands with the holy oils and bound them with the linen maniple, an ornamental vestment worn on the arm. I looked towards Mom in the second pew and was so filled with joy that I thought my heart would burst. There is no more emotional moment in an Irish man's life than to give his first priestly blessing to his mom and have her kiss his blessed hands. Years later, as is also the tradition with Irish priests and their mothers, my ordination maniple would be placed in her coffin when she was buried.

Sensing that Dad was tired after milking cows and driving 110 miles to attend, I helped him kneel as he approached me for his blessing. As expected, he was silent, but the look on his face said what I needed to hear and echoed with the bishop's words of ordination declaring that, in the tradition of priests centuries before me, I was now a priest forever according to the order of Melchisedech.

Chapter 5

The New Priest

On the day following ordination day, my relatives and friends joined me at St. Michael's Church in Potahee for my first mass. Even though I had practiced the rubrics of how the priest should hold his hands and genuflect properly, I was nervous. I was awed that I, a sinner, was going to say the words of consecration over bread and wine and turn them into the body and blood of Jesus Christ.

Mary Beatty nee Farrelly was now sacristan. When I entered the sacristy with my new alb over my arm, she gave me her usual bear hug. With tears in her eyes, she said she hoped I liked the flowers on the altar, as they were from her own garden. I cheered Mary up by recalling the time when, as a boy serving Mass, I served barefooted because I had forgotten my sneakers. She laughed and said, "You have come a long way since you were a boy of ten. And I can still picture you a baby rocking yourself to sleep in the cradle in Legaginney."

My homily at the mass was brief, and was followed by an individual blessing to each person in the church full of people. The members of our summer football and dance gang were the last to approach the altar rails for my blessing. Brian Smith had a smile from ear to ear. He grabbed my hands as I finished the blessing, kissed them, and said, "God bless you, Father Finbarr."

Next to Brian, Barney Brody knelt with his head down. I guess he was thinking of what he said six years before: "It will be awful if you are ever a priest." I gave him my blessing and grabbed his cheeks. We both had tears in our eyes.

As was typical for all newly ordained priests in Ireland, my family, friends and all the locals in and around Legaginney treated me like royalty before I left for America. With the monetary gifts, I bought a second-hand car, a beautiful black Austin 40. There were several parties at Legaginney. Mom played the violin and Fr. Jim Daly, the Yankee priest, had us all in stitches as he sang "Paddy McGinty's Goat." My brother Jack must have told Fr. Jim about Mom's aversion to alcohol, because neither he nor Jack did any serious drinking at these parties.

Dad, always the gracious host, asked Fr. Jim if there was any special place in Ireland that he would like to visit. We had plenty of drivers around, since everybody on the farm in Legaginney was taking a week's vacation in my honor. Fr. Jim enthusiastically replied, "Mr. Corr, I would love to visit friends in Portumna, County Galway."

Without hesitation, Dad said, "I know it very well. I spent three months in prison there." Poor Fr. Jim looked perplexed. Jack roared with laughter, as he had jokingly said to Fr. Jim on the boat over to Ireland, "My father should have stayed in prison as Nell would have done a better job raising us nine kids." What he hadn't told Fr. Jim then was that Dad was very proud of the time he spent in prison as a captured IRA soldier.

I felt bad for the poor Yankee priest and later explained to him that from 1919–1921 Dad had served as a volunteer soldier in the cause of Irish freedom against the British crown. While Dad forbade any of

51

his sons to join the IRA, he was secretly very proud of having been part of liberating the southern twenty-six counties of Ireland from British tyranny. Dad had been imprisoned twice and, at one point, had gone on a hunger strike for over two weeks. Later I drove Fr. Jim to Portumna to visit his friends. We had a great time, but we didn't visit Portumna prison.

My two months of vacation rushed by. I reveled in the many parties and weddings that I was invited to attend. Being Irish, I was not surprised that before one of these weddings Murphy's Law intervened - if something can go wrong, it will and, not only that, it will go wrong at the worst possible time. Miriam, the bride, had asked me to drive her to visit a mutual friend in the town of Monaghan twenty-five miles away. Because of all my social engagements, I was frequently observing Irish time, which meant that I was usually thirty minutes to one hour late. Miriam wasn't impressed that the rest of the community was worshiping me. As I approached, she was standing outside her mother's teashop with fire in her eyes. No "Good day, Father" came from Miriam's mouth. She threw her bag into the back seat and scowled, "Mary will be worried that we are over an hour late. Let's go."

Now my Irish was up. I said to myself, "Miriam, you are going to get one hell of a fast ride this evening." I sped out of town at sixty mph, not taking into account that the roads could be treacherous after the summer squall that had just ended. Near St. Pat's College, I hit the brakes suddenly to maneuver around a sharp bend.

We didn't make it. My Austin 40 did a complete 180-degree skid and slid backwards into the ditch. At first I was relieved that no one was hurt and that it didn't seem I had done too much damage to my car. I was more embarrassed when several people stopped to help. I kept wondering, "What are they thinking as they see this newly ordained priest, in full clerical dress, sitting with his legs in the air beside this stunningly beautiful woman?" To add to all the embarrassment, the tow truck driver who pulled us out of the ditch was a Protestant and must have wondered about finding a young priest in such a delicate situation.

Miriam had one minor casualty. The mechanic tore her pantyhose as he was pulling her out of the bushes. I thought to myself, "Miriam, you cannot blame me for the hole in your pantyhose." As my mechanical savior took my Austin 40 for a trial run before we set off again for Monaghan, it became obvious that only the muffler was broken. Miriam and I resumed our journey, this time with more caution, a loud roar, and torn pantyhose. Up until that time, I had not agreed to attend her wedding. As we drove along, we didn't talk much because of the noise. She did, however, yell at me, "After all this, you will now come to my wedding." I said, "Sure, but don't tell your groom. I will use this whole incident as part of my toast at the wedding reception."

When I took my car to a local garage the next day and parked the car on the side of a hill, I forgot to pull the brake. The car rolled slowly down the hill and into the garage, to the surprise of the three mechanics inside. While they repaired the car, I went shopping in a ladies store for a pair of pantyhose. The shopkeeper assumed that I was a Protestant minister. She asked, "Reverend, what size does your wife wear?" Without blinking an eyelid, I said, "Medium long."

I participated in Miriam's wedding a month later. The groom had a good sense of humor, thank God. My toast was, "Here is to Miriam, who spent an evening in a ditch with a newly ordained priest." As the groom sat startled, I told the whole story and ended it by saying how much easier it was to replace pantyhose and a muffler than a beautiful bride.

As with all good things, the joy-filled summer came to an end. I bought my airline ticket to fly from Dublin to what was then Idlewild Airport in New York City. The folks around Legaginney gave me a going away party at which several of the locals sang songs and recalled many humorous stories about the boy Finbarr, now Fr. Finbarr, on his way to the missions in America. As usual, Miss Berrill sang:

Goodbye, Johnny dear, when you're far away,
Don't forget your dear old mother far across the sea.
Write a letter now and then and send her all you can,
And don't forget where e'er you roam that you're an
Irishman.

Mom was in tears. She had nurtured me for twenty-five years, and now she felt that the seeds she had sown during those years had come to fruition since I would convert many Americans to the Catholic Church. She reassured me that her tears were tears of joy for me. She expressed her unshakeable conviction that I would make a big difference in America. Twenty of my family and friends made a caravan of cars and accompanied me, the brave young missionary, to the airport. As customary with the Irish, they avoided talking about the fact that I was leaving them, probably never to return to live permanently in Ireland.

I made my tearful farewells and passed through customs one hour before flight time. But Murphy's Law struck again. Just as I was seated and had fastened my seatbelt, the captain announced that lights on the plane weren't working and that all passengers would have to disembark. I knew that everybody except Dad would still be there waiting to see the plane take off. I decided to make the best of it and turn lemons into lemonade. Swaggering off the plane as if I were a John Wayne cowboy, I put on the best American accent I could imagine, talking through my nose as if I had already spent several years in New Jersey.

I approached Mom, who was already laughing her eyes out, and asked her to introduce me to the family and friends, saying, "I've been away so long." To younger relatives like Fetim Corr, I commented, "Oh how you have grown." Two hours later, the captain called us back aboard. This time, I left with much laughter and no tears. When I said my Divine Office on the plane, I thanked God for a beautiful family and for friends who supported me in my journey towards the priesthood. I also thanked God for keeping my pure in thought and action during my first two months as a priest.

My first shock upon arriving in the United States on August 20th was the tremendous heat and humidity. It was 85 degrees at midnight. Translating that to the daytime temperature, I expected it to be 120 degrees by midday. My first cousin Alice, who was a court stenographer with good connections, managed to get a pass to meet me in the customs area. I was already learning that "it is not how much you know in America that really matters – it's whom you know." If the heat wasn't enough, my next shock was having my neck and hands bitten by a hoard of mosquitoes, insects rare in Ireland. They didn't seem to bother Cousin Alice, who laughed and said, "The mosquitoes are after the greenhorn."

Alice's parents, Uncle Joe Corr and Aunt Molly, greeted me with warm hugs. I remembered Uncle Joe's generosity when, on his visit to Ireland years back, he had thrilled me by stuffing the enormous sum of a five-pound note into my pocket. This time I was thrilled because they had a window air conditioner. They suggested that I would possibly be cooler if I took off my black woolen suit jacket and Roman collar.

Bursting with excitement about meeting my hero Fr. Michael the next day, I hardly slept at all that night. On the way through Manhattan the next morning, I once again felt like the little boy from the country. I stared out the windows at the mighty skyscrapers and the majestic St. Patrick's Cathedral on Fifth Avenue. I thought that the Con Edison sign at one of the crosswalks, "Dig we must for a growing New York," was humorous. Coming through the Lincoln Tunnel and driving to East Orange, New Jersey during commuter time was a nightmare, and we were delayed for two hours. I learned very quickly that one of Fr. Michael's obsessions was being on time. The first thing that he said when we arrived was, "Joe, you are late as usual." Joe ignored his comment and said, "Don't you want to welcome your nephew, Fr. Finbarr, to New Jersey?"

Fr. Michael was just as I had pictured him. He was over six-feet tall, with perfect gait and snow-white hair. As you might expect from an army chaplain who had personally thrown hand grenades at the Germans during the war, heroics that earned him six Medals of Honor, he was not an openly affectionate person. Yet I could feel his love when he said, "We will have to get you a light summer suit tomorrow."

I slept well that night, but was awakened by an odd, repetitive screech from the kitchen. "Good morning, Father Corr:" the voice sounded German, but it didn't sound human. I was right on both guesses. It was a parrot trained by Sophie, the German cook, to greet my uncle as he came to eat after early morning mass.

After breakfast Uncle Mike and I departed on our search for my new suit. The little Jewish tailor smiled when we entered his shop. My uncle, quick to business, announced, "I want the lightest and best black suit in the house for my nephew, who has just emigrated to America." The tailor showed us a beautiful black jacket and pants. The jacket fit perfectly. Even though the tailor offered to put cuffs on the pants for free, my uncle still asked, "How about the ten-percent clergy discount?"

What a relief to get out of the black wool! When my brother Jack came to take me to his rectory in Morristown for the weekend, he said, "You already look like a native in your black serge suit." Before I left East Orange, Fr. Michael also told me that his old 1949 Chevrolet would be mine as soon as I was settled and had a driver's license.

My weekend at Assumption Parish with Jack was uneventful, except for the fact that he invited me to perform the Sunday baptisms. I agreed before I discovered there were eight babies on that particular Sunday. I decided then that, if I ever found myself stationed in a big parish like Assumption in Morristown, I would have twelve or so pacifiers hidden with the baptismal oils. Eight crying babies drove me nuts, but at least the parents and godparents appreciated my cute brogue.

Later, Jack took me around to meet the local priests. Msgr. Sheerin, who served both as pastor of St. Margaret's of Scotland Morristown and as assistant to the bishop, welcomed me warmly. He had the reputation of being very crusty, but had a deep affection for priests, especially if they were Irish. He said as we were leaving, "If you ever need me, just call." Msgr. Hill, rector of the Cathedral, who loved to challenge young priests asked, "Finbarr, what are you doing in America? Why didn't you stay at home in Ireland and help your mother?" I was ready for him. I answered boldly, "I felt that God was calling me to the missions." He answered with a big grin, "I like that you are spunky. You will do well in this country."

As I expected, Fr. Jim Daly had great fun introducing me to his friends. On his day off he took me to meet his sister Esther, who treated him like an errant schoolboy and chastised him for having a soiled shirt. Both she and her husband Charlie were great cooks, and invited me to come for meals as often as I wished. My first faux pas was that week when Fr. Jim took me to meet his Italian friends Al and Rae Scala, the first Italian family to invite me to dinner. To me, practically starved to death during eleven years in boarding school, the meal seemed an orgy of antipasto, soup, salad, lasagna, and cheesecake. When leaving that evening, I felt very much part of the Scala family. I thanked all with a firm shake of the hand and, when Mrs. Scala came forward to give me a warm embrace, I automatically did what I would do with any girl I had danced with in Ireland and patted her on the rear. She roared with laughter, saying, "Oh, he pats ladies on the

PoPo." They all laughed, but Fr. Jim told me as we drove off, "You cannot do that in America, and if you do, you will get yourself in trouble."

My second faux pas was the following week when Fr. Jim took me to a dinner for some local priests at the home of Msgr. Steffen, a giant man of Polish extraction. The big monsignor apologized that, this being the cook's day off, we would have to put up with his attempt at cooking. After salad, he carried a big black pot to the center of the dining room table and began to dish out some long stringy stuff that reminded me of raw pig guts from the farm in Legaginney. I was ready to vomit. Looking at me with a smile, he said, "Does the greenhorn like spaghetti?" I said, "I don't know. I've never had it."

While the native priests were covering the spaghetti with a red sauce that looked like blood, I reached for the French dressing and spread it over my serving. It didn't taste that awful until my newly adopted brothers in the priesthood started laughing and told me that French dressing was for the salad only and that the red stuff was made from tomatoes and other ingredients. That evening I would have much preferred Nell Corr's chicken, cabbage, and potatoes.

During dinner the good monsignor confided that he had a copy of the assignments for the newly ordained. He agreed to share the details if we kept everything a secret until the letters were mailed the following Tuesday. Looking at me, he announced, "Finbarr, you are to report to Msgr. Murphy at St. Agnes Church in Paterson on September 4th at twelve noon."

Fr. Jim jumped with joy. "That is my native parish. Finbarr, you lucky Irishman! You are going to be near my sister Esther and her husband Charlie, which, Fr.

Jim knew, meant that a good Irish meal would always be within my reach when nothing else seemed edible.

Chapter 6

St. Agnes Parish

Bishop McNulty's appointment letter in hand, I arrived at St. Agnes' rectory in Paterson in early September of 1960. Jack drove me over to St. Agnes. As we approached, I noticed much more garbage on the sides of the road than I had seen at my brother Jack's parish in Morristown. Weeds and grass grew from cracks in the sidewalks. The children playing in the backyards seemed much poorer, and there was a larger Hispanic and Black population than I had seen in Morristown. I immediately felt needed, much more so than if I had been assigned to a parish full of millionaires.

Msgr. Murphy was on vacation, so his associate Fr. Wolsin greeted me, the new curate from Ireland. He did so warmly and invited my brother Jack to stay for lunch with us. I soon had my first shock. Louise, a buxom blonde who had served many years as parish secretary, greeted me in the dining room with a big, wet kiss right on the lips. I immediately thought of Holy Tom's warning in the seminary, "Watch out for those sexy blondes in America."

My bedroom was my office, and I shared the bathroom with Fr. Wolsin. The parish comprised 650 families of Irish, Italian, and German extraction. The Catholic grammar school had an enrollment of 300 students and was administered and taught by the Sisters of Charity. The sisters were delighted to have a young priest stationed at the parish, as they felt that both Msgr. Murphy and Fr. Wolsin had become burned out by working with children and teenagers over too many years.

On Sunday morning Fr. Wolsin warmly introduced me at all the masses. With a great sense of humor, he asked the parishioners to pray for him because, as a person of Polish descent, he didn't know how he would cope with both an Irish pastor and now a junior Irish curate. Wolsin and I had formed a strong bond before Msgr. Murphy returned from vacation one week later.

Murphy didn't have Wolsin's sensitivity to a greenhorn priest who was 4,000 miles away from home for the first time. He did try to make me feel welcome by introducing me to several of his lay friends, who took me to my first ice hockey game at Madison Square Garden. But he was very controlling and insisted that I ask permission to leave the rectory to do the smallest of errands, such as going downtown to buy a new pair of shoes. He also wanted me to reimburse him for any personal phone calls I made to my nearby relatives.

Marge, the rectory cook, was a diminutive woman partly crippled from polio as a child. She was delighted to have a skinny priest to fatten up. During the first week, she asked pleadingly, "Did they feed you guys anything at all in the seminary?" When I told her that our daily diet was porridge for breakfast, two slices of bread with jam for lunch, and steamed meat, cabbage, and potatoes for supper, she was aghast.

Each day Marge served a scrumptious breakfast of bacon, eggs, and toast. Lunch was a delicious stew or a juicy hamburger with French fries. Dinner was always a specialty like leg of lamb or stuffed chicken, with an appetizing fish dinner on Fridays, of course. In the seminary we were never certain if there would be any food left when the dish came back around, so I had developed the bad habit of piling my plate very high. The housekeeper, who served the meals at St. Agnes, would report me to Marge, who then trudged out from the kitchen to remind me that there was plenty of food. According to Marge, because three meals a day were not enough for an emaciated young priest, at ten o'clock each evening she would fix me a sandwich the size of a doorstep and serve it with a glass of milk.

In addition to carrying my share of daily masses, administering the sacraments, and hearing confessions, I ministered to the youth of the parish. To better understand their parents, I asked Msgr. Murphy for permission to conduct a census. Did I ever get an education! In Ireland ninety-nine percent of the population attended church weekly, and couples were validly married. In Paterson I was shocked to discover that many of the parishioners attended mass perhaps twice a year at most. Several couples were in common-law marriages or had been married for a second time by a justice of the peace. Using my Irish charm and sense of humor, I invited the lapsed Catholics to return and promised that I would not judge them if they chose to confess to me as part of their journey back.

My second shock at St. Agnes Parish came on one of those census trips. I had climbed to the third floor of an apartment building on Main Street and knocked on the door to ask if any Catholics resided there. The lady who opened the door must have been expecting her husband or a boyfriend, but clearly not her parish priest in full clericals. She was totally naked down to her waist. I must confess that it was difficult for me to keep looking at her eyes and not at her breasts. Showing no sign of embarrassment, she simply said, with a Spanish accent, "We no longer are Catholic. We go to the Pentecostal Church." I mumbled "Thank you" and went home to say my prayers.

This experience should have prepared me for the sensitive situation in which I next found myself. Before mass, I had just finished a premarital session with the first couple whose marriage I would witness. Karen and George were delightful and presented no real challenge. I was comfortable discussing all the legal and moral requirements for a valid sacrament in the Catholic Church. Since I wanted my first married couple to be perfectly prepared and happy, I asked, "Karen and George, are there any other questions you are worried about? If I don't know the answer, I will look it up." Without batting an eye, Karen said, "Since we are both Catholic, would it be a sin if my husband kisses my breasts when we make love?" Thank God they didn't realize that I was aroused by her question. Still distracted after they had departed, I forgot to light the candles at the mass that was next on my schedule.

I was very comfortable with children and teenagers. I visited the Catholic grammar school frequently and assisted with the religious education of the public school students who attended our weekly Catholic Christian Doctrine (CCD) classes. The biggest challenge was the religious formation of the public school students. Since the teenagers had already received the sacrament of Confirmation, neither the parents nor the students themselves felt any moral obligation to attend the CCD classes. Not accepting this state of affairs, I seized the opportunity when it was my turn to preach at all the masses. I accused seventy-five percent of the parents of not keeping their marital vows. That got their attention. In the course of my sermon, I explained the rationale for my accusation. Since only twenty-five percent of public school students attended CCD classes, the parents of the other seventy-five percent were in default of their promise made at their marriage to educate their children in the Catholic faith.

Everybody was shocked at my sermon. Wolsin took me aside and gently told me, "Finbarr, in America we don't usually attack the parishioners as you just did. We invite the parents to act responsibly." I could tell by his tone of voice that he really liked my youthful enthusiasm, as he offered to help me form a board of directors for the high school CCD. The board and I agreed that students would not be allowed to attend the CCD social program of dances led by a disc jockey unless they also attended the CCD educational classes. To build interest, we invited all the teenagers to one opening dance with a very popular disc jockey known for featuring the latest Beatles music.

The occasion was a great success. Ninety teenagers came to rock and roll almost to exhaustion. I was appalled that the boys and girls were draped all over each other on the dance floor. Sensitized to the need to be diplomatic, I tapped the closely dancing couples on the shoulder, and said, "Why don't you pull back a little and leave place for the Holy Ghost." Some of the kids shot back at me, "Do you think we are having sex on the dance floor?" Others just smiled and thought my instruction was cute. Wolsin thought it very funny, and said, "The Irish really have their hang-ups on sex."

Wolsin and I became fast friends and started to work as a team. Msgr. Murphy wasn't too happy because now he had to deal with not just one but two popular curates. While other priests took offense at Fr. Wolsin imitating my brogue, I interpreted it as flattery. On one occasion, he answered the phone with his Finbarr brogue and faked it so adeptly that the woman parishioner, who knew me well, thought she was speaking to me.

For Halloween the school's Home & School Association planned a costume party. Murphy dressed as a cowboy, Wolsin as a jailbird, and I went as a blood donor. I painted my whole face and my arms in white except for my nose, which was red. I wore pajamas and bathrobe and hung a sign around my neck that said, "I want to give my last pint of blood." I received first prize for the most creative costume. Murphy thought my outfit was obscene.

On nights like this Wolsin loved to take the microphone and tell stories to the parishioners. I was often the target of his humor. One particular night he moaned how difficult it was to share a bathroom with an Irishman, claiming that I had brought a goat from Ireland with me and that I housed it in the common bathroom. Fr. Wolsin reported to the audience that he had complained to the bishop about the smell of the goat but didn't get much help. According to Wolsin, the bishop's only response was to ask him, "Why don't you just open the window of the bathroom?" Wolsin replied, "And let out my pigeons?"

My first winter in America was difficult. I was not accustomed to the high temperature and dryness from indoor heating. Between confessions, without bothering to put a coat on, I would rush outside gasping for fresh air. I ended up in bed for four days with a flu and high fever. Rose, the housekeeper, brought me chicken soup, and Wolsin checked on me frequently. Murphy didn't want to visit me because he was worried that he might catch the flu.

Even in this situation, Wolsin couldn't resist teasing me. Because he had served as spiritual director to an actors' guild in New York City, he had many young friends from the entertainment industry. One of these budding young talents was Florence Henderson, who later became a major television star. Florence had stopped to see Wolsin, and he decided that it would be a good joke to have her lie down beside me in bed while I slept. Then he woke me with, "What are you doing with a film star in your bed?"

Christmas 1960 was my first Christmas away from home. I received many cards and beautiful gifts. One parish couple gave me a beautiful card with two twenty-dollar bills enclosed with the message "Merry Christmas. We are proud of our Irish curate." I was in total shock, as that money amounted to almost twenty-five percent of my monthly salary. The three priests celebrated a solemn high mass, and the choir's beautiful songs made me feel as though I were on the mountains above Bethlehem with the shepherds, listening to the choirs of Angels welcoming the baby Jesus in the manger.

As the choir sang "Silent Night" and all lights except for those at the crib were turned down, I cried silently. I longed to be in Legaginney just for fifteen minutes to wish my family a Happy Christmas. As mass ended, families hugged each other and wished everybody a Merry Christmas. Although I had nobody special to hug, I did have Christmas dinner with Fr. Jim's sister Esther.

After only four months it was clear that Msgr. Murphy was increasingly jealous of my popularity. I was the first Irish-born priest stationed there in ten years, so parishioners were intrigued and entertained by my Irish brogue. They liked my sense of humor and my use of it to engage the young people in the parish.

My relationship with Murphy came to a head after he returned from one of his frequent vacations in his typical ornery mood. In the best of times, Wolsin and I didn't look forward to Murphy's return and usually had a lot more fun when he was away. This time, when Murphy returned to learn that the church sexton, Larry, was doing chores for me instead of keeping the parking lots free of snow, he hit the roof.

After listening to Murphy scream at me, I was sitting down having a good cry for myself when Wolsin came in through our common bathroom to learn what all the screaming was about. When I told him of Murphy's outburst, he grabbed me and said, unknowingly echoing my mother's affirmation to me when I was only twelve, "Remember, you didn't come to America to serve Murphy, but to serve God." He added, "One day, Finbarr, you are going to make a big difference in the diocese of Paterson."

Even with Marge's delicious meals, I remained a skinny 170 pounds. I had several colds with a terribly sore throat that first winter and was nagged by the parish staff to go to the doctor. After looking into my mouth for two minutes, the doctor pronounced, "You are never going to gain any weight as long as you have those rotten tonsils."

The operation was successful, but I wasn't very impressed when Dr. Connelly used gauze to stuff the hole where my tonsils had been and left a string hanging out of my mouth. When I asked him what the string was for, he just said, "If you are getting a feeling you are going to choke, just pull the string." That same night I unknowingly pulled the string while I was asleep. I began to hemorrhage like a stuck pig, and the bed quickly filled with blood. Dr. Connolly was called at 2 A.M. to come rescue me from bleeding to death.

When I awoke the next morning, Wolsin was at my bedside. Smiling, he held out the teddy bear he was holding and said, "Every little boy getting his tonsils out should have a teddy bear." When I returned to the rectory, the three ladies at the rectory had a welcoming home party for the recovering patient. Marge was relieved to hear me speak. She had worried that Dr. Connolly would remove my brogue along with the tonsils.

My relationship with Murphy continued to deteriorate, but to my complete surprise, my prayers were answered in June of 1961 when Murphy announced his transfer to a big parish three miles up the road. Wolsin and I could barely suppress our enthusiasm and decided to celebrate the occasion. Our sense of celebration was short-lived, however. Wolsin was called to the bishop's office that same week to learn that he was appointed pastor of a little parish twenty miles north.

That was the week for surprises, but the best was yet to come. Fr. Jim Daly called me on Friday, and said, "How would you like me to be your new pastor?" I didn't believe it would be possible for him to become pastor of small St. Agnes after having been pastor of a bigger parish. I said, "Jim, don't pull my leg on this one. I don't want to believe you and then find myself disappointed." He said, "Call my sister Esther. You know she wouldn't lie. I don't know if I can stand being a pastor there, if she and Charlie still attend St. Agnes. She will be getting her nose into everything and bugging me."

I did notice that Jim wasn't the usual jovial priest who had attended my ordination in Ireland. I learned later that the bishop had become aware of his drinking problem and was moving him closer to the bishop's office to keep a closer eye on him. I was thrilled, as I knew that Fr. Jim loved me like a brother and would give me much more freedom than Murphy.

Esther was angry with the bishop for demoting her brother, but she was also happy that he was stationed with me. She hoped that my total abstinence from alcohol would have a positive influence on his tendency to over imbibe. Esther took the pressure off him by announcing that she would switch parishes.

On the day Fr. Jim moved in he called me into his office and said, pointing to the phone, "Finbarr, call your parents in Ireland and tell them who your new pastor is." I answered, a little embarrassed, "Mom and Dad don't have a phone, but I have already written to them about the good news." Even though Fr. Jim was technically my boss, he treated me as a peer. Since I was now driving Uncle Mike's old '49 Chevy, I did most of the driving when we went down the New Jersey shore for Irish night at Jimmy Byrne's nightclub, or to Morristown, or to visit Fr. Jim's friends in the old parish in Boonton.

Fr. Jim kept a low profile in the parish for the first few months. Like me, he had great devotion to the Blessed Mother. He packed the church on every Monday night by initiating a Miraculous Medal Novena in honor of the Blessed Virgin. He gave me freedom to expand the youth ministry to include basketball, track, trips to the Jersey shore, and hay rides. Unlike Murphy, he wasn't threatened by my popularity.

On St. Patrick's Day, which had a great tradition at St. Agnes Parish, I preached a homily I had received from Uncle Mike on the marks of Irish Catholicism that make it unique. I expounded on Ireland's devotion to the Blessed Trinity (Father, Son, and Holy Ghost) and to the Virgin Mary, and to its love of the Mass and respect for the pope. In the meantime, the social committee worried that Fr. Jim's apparent depression would be a damper on the St. Patrick's dinner and social to follow. They challenged him to get into the spirit of the day's celebration party: "You need to take the poker down your ass before the party. The priests of the parish always get into the spirit of the party. What are you going to do?"

Fair play to him, Fr. Jim took the criticism on the chin and decided to meet the challenge. With the help of the sexton and a parishioner, we prepared a skit for the parish party called "Ireland's Answer to the Beatles." With fake guitars, green wigs, and borrowed tuxedos, we brought down the house.

Fr. Jim became both my mentor and a close friend. Whenever I did make mistakes, as most young priests do, he would defend me publicly before my accusers, yet only admonish me in private. Once I spanked a teenager for throwing an egg into the school auditorium on Mischief Night. When the teen's father came to the rectory and threatened civil action, Fr. Jim defended me, saying, "Sir, you have to understand that Fr. Finbarr is a very devoted young priest who loves teenagers. Don't you feel your son contributed to this altercation?" The father left with his tail between his legs. Privately, Father Jim warned me, "You are going to get yourself in trouble with the law. It is illegal to administer physical punishment in America."

After the successful St. Patrick's party, Fr. Jim began to relax and would invite friends over to the rectory for a drink. One night we blew up two plastic legs, put the buxom secretary Louise's shoes on the feet, and placed the legs so that that protruded out from under his bed. As the guests went from his study to the toilet through the bedroom, they couldn't help but notice the legs. The women in particular would shriek as they beheld what they thought was one of the guests out cold under the bed.

By midnight at these parties, I would be tired of drinking Coca Cola and smoking Pall Malls, so I would attempt to get away to bed. Standing solemnly by the door with my arms by my side, Fr. Jim would ask, "What is the problem now?" I would answer, "Just because we have company, you won't kiss me goodnight." The guests would howl and then I would proceed to tell the story about the pastor who turned in his new assistant to the bishop with the complaint, "Bishop, the new assistant you sent me is gay." "How do you know?" the bishop would ask. "I certainly know," says the pastor, "because he giggled when I kissed him goodnight."

Before going to bed, I always reminded Jim to let the air out of the plastic legs and hide them under the mattress. I knew that our Irish housekeeper Kathleen, who was from County Limerick, would not appreciate any such shenanigans going on in a priest's bedroom. One time Fr. Jim remembered to hide the legs, but he left Louise's shoes under the bed. Everything seemed in order the next morning until Kathleen went up to make Fr. Jim's bed as usual while he was celebrating mass. Upon her discovery of the shoes under his bed, all hell broke loose. Pots and pans flew in the kitchen. Kathleen was yelling, "Celibacy be damned. How can a priest be celibate when he has the secretary's shoes under his bed?" I was persuaded to be the mediator on the presumption that Kathleen would respect a fellow Irishman. Something had to be done because our lunch was at stake. We got our lunch, but Kathleen never did see the humor of the situation.

I enjoyed working with Fr. Jim and tried not to take advantage of his kindness. I would sometimes stay out at a party in New York until the wee hours. When he would ask what time I had gotten home the previous night, he would good-naturedly accept my playful and vague replies like "Plenty after midnight."

One night I quietly tiptoed in about 1 A.M., walking carefully past his door to avoid the creaky boards. As I turned the bedroom light on, I was caught off guard by the plastic legs and Louise's shoes protruding from beneath my bed. This time I was the one shrieking. Pretending that he had been asleep, Fr. Jim rushed to me with mock concern, "Finbarr, are you alright?" He then retreated to his bedroom with his customary giggle.

Over time I became more involved in activities outside the parish. Brian Smith, my colleague from Legaginney School, was now playing Irish football with a club in the Bronx. I became chaplain to the club and was invited to all their parties and dances. I am sure it was my sense of humor, more than good looks, which made many of the girls want to dance with me. It was undeniably enjoyable, but I knew I was flirting with danger. When I would get up to say mass the next morning, I would feel guilty even though nothing really physical had taken place between me and any of the ladies.

I discussed the matter with my Jesuit spiritual director. I explained that I was tired of being an extrovert and the center of attention at these parties, as I felt it was eventually going to get me in serious trouble. I told him my plan was to withdraw and become an introvert. He disagreed strongly and asked, "How many converts to Catholicism have you had this past year?" I answered, "Eleven." He replied, "God called you just as you are to be his priest. He wants to use all of you, and that includes your charm and your Irish humor to do His ministry."

I did have one truly frightening experience at St. Agnes rectory. Louise called me to my office to meet with an unidentified lady who had asked to talk with a priest. The woman, attractive and with a Marilyn Monroe-sexy voice, opened the conversation by asking me very personal questions about my age and background before the seminary. I tried to be evasive and polite. Suddenly she said, "I have taken care of young priest's sexual needs before, and by the way, I don't have anything on under the raincoat."

Sweating, I talked very loudly to draw the attention of Louise, who was in her office next door. Louise rushed to the door to inquire, "Father Finbarr, do you need any help?" The lady in the raincoat bolted out of the room. Once again, I said to myself, "My mother's prayers are saving me."

I don't know what it was that attracted people to me for individual counseling. I blamed Fr. Wolsin because many people who had sought his counsel had nowhere to turn when he left. They turned to me with the hope that I had his skills. I missed him and the fun we had together at St. Agnes.

He loved to tell the story of how one time the two of us volunteered to remove snow at the bishop's residence in Paterson. The bishop wasn't around, and we didn't bother to introduce ourselves to the two German nuns in charge at the residence. One of them assumed that we were recovering alcoholics from the Straight and Narrow Rehab Center in Paterson. She said, "I would like to offer you a drink, but I know you can't have any." Wolsin kept an absolutely straight face and replied, "That's right, Sister. We Irish have a little problem with the drink. Thank you, Sister, for the thought." Obviously the joke was meant for me, even though I was still a total abstainer.

As time went on, the diocese recognized that I had more talent that could be shared outside St. Agnes Parish. I was appointed to teach theology at DePaul High School in Wayne, New Jersey, which I really enjoyed. I was also invited to serve on the diocesan vocation committee, and was appointed Assistant Director of the diocesan Family Life Bureau. Because I already had trouble fending off clients' transference towards me and controlling my own attraction to some of my clients, I very eagerly accepted an invitation from Bishop Casey to take courses in pastoral counseling at Seton Hall University.

Other than my ordination to the priesthood, I don't know of anything that caused such an epiphany in my life as my experience of studying psychology at Seton Hall. My greater awareness of how feelings affected my life and my relationships at St. Agnes Parish opened the door to new worlds and new experiences. I came as a boy to St. Agnes in 1960. Now, in 1966, I was an adult.

Chapter 7

Ma Haag

I didn't return to Ireland during my first years at St. Agnes. To be totally honest, I didn't have enough money. The monthly salary and stipends were only $300 per month. Since my parents were getting older and probably wouldn't be coming to America any time soon, I saved enough for a trip home each summer. I was due to visit home again in August 1966. Fr. Jim usually took the month of July off and visited friends at the Jersey shore. This particular summer he stayed close to Paterson. He must have had a premonition that I would soon be transferred to another parish since I had already been at St. Agnes for six years.

I didn't relish a transfer. I had made many good friends who invited me to be part of their family celebrations. Some of the older women like Nora Quintevella, herself a native of County Mayo, pampered me as though I were a son. Nora would do all my Christmas shopping for me and wrap thirty gifts to take home to my relatives in Ireland.

I loved my ministry to youth and had become a surrogate father to young boys and girls whose fathers had disappeared after divorcing their mothers. I knew I should move on to new challenges, but I was afraid to part from this spiritual family who had loved and nurtured me. They also had protected me from the young widow and the attractive single adult women who believed that Fr. Finbarr needed more than just spiritual affection.

Prior to the Second Vatican Council, all personnel matters at the bishop's office were dealt with in utmost secrecy. Furthermore, priests both young and old were expected to accept new assignments without prior consultation. In spite of all that, rumors started flying in June of 1966. Fr. Jim went to lunch in mid-June with a priest connected to the powers-that-be in the bishop's office. The priest swore Jim to secrecy, and then said, "Jim, I'm sorry to tell you that Finbarr is going to be transferred to Monsignor 'Mother' Haag in Morristown."

When Jim phoned from the restaurant, his slurred words told me that he had been drinking. He was struggling to hold back the tears. "You are going, but I cannot tell you where. Vera, the bishop's secretary, has put the letters in the mail. You can go to the post office and pick yours up at ten o'clock tonight." He added, "I'll see you later."

He didn't return to the rectory that afternoon. To pass the time and relieve the pain, I played baseball with some of the teenagers. As the assistant postmaster handed me the bishop's letter that night, he said, "I hope it is good news." I decided not to open the letter at that time, just in case it was a transfer to a terrible assignment. I thought to myself, "Surely Jim will be home to console me." He was home all right, but he was in no shape to help anybody. I found him stretched out on his bed outside the covers. He had obviously been drinking since lunchtime. "Jim, Jim," I said, "can I talk to you?" All I heard was a few grunts. I retreated to my own suite and opened the letter slowly. "You will report to Monsignor Christian D. Haag on Friday on August 1st at twelve noon".

Still sad, I stared at the bishop's letter on my desk for two whole days. Finally, Msgr. Haag called. Very positive and excited, he asked if there was anything he could do to make my transition easier. I replied, "Yes. I have already booked a trip to Ireland to visit my family, and I planned to leave on August 8th." He agreed immediately that I should proceed with my plans, and added, "We'll have a bon voyage party for you before you go."

With mixed feelings, I packed my few belongings and books in the old wooden trunk and drove west on Route 46 to Morristown. This time I was ready. If any sexy blonde attempted to kiss me, she was going to get my cheek, not my Irish lips. I was a little worried when I discovered that Ma Haag's other curate was also both being replaced at the same time. The other newcomer was a shy, newly ordained curate named Richard Olivieri.

In my new assignment, I discovered too quickly that, even though Ma Haag had a wonderful reputation throughout the diocese, he left many gaps in parish administration. I had been there only two days when a representative of the State of New Jersey called and asked by name for the priest I had just replaced. Stepping into my new role, I greeted the official, who immediately attacked me, saying, "Don't you know, Father, that you are breaking the law by being behind in paying withholding tax on parish employees?" Not even knowing what withholding tax was, I said nothing. He added, "This is a civil offense, punishable by a fine and imprisonment."

My Irish up, I pleaded, "Mister, have a heart. I have barely unpacked my bags or settled in here. May I have Msgr. Haag send you a check today?" Haag laughed first and apologized to me only later. As I said my prayers that night, I said to myself, "I would much more have preferred to have a sexy blonde kiss me on the lips than to have a civil official from the state threaten to imprison me as soon as I arrived at St. Margaret's of Scotland Parish."

The bon voyage party showed that Haag was more astute at planning parties than paying taxes. He invited twenty of my best friends from St. Agnes Parish along with several staff members from St. Margaret's. The big cake was decorated with an airplane with the inscription "Fr. Finbarr is up, up and away." I departed for Ireland on August 8th secure in the knowledge that I could work well with him.

Fr. Olivieri, "Ritchie" to those of us in the rectory, turned out to be a quick and charming colleague. He enjoyed working in the background, organizing liturgies, and visiting the sick while Haag and I were busy with the public relations work. About this time, I had started studying for a master's degree in pastoral counseling at Ionia College in New Rochelle. Each Friday morning I drove the fifty-five miles to New Rochelle, leaving the parish responsibility to Ma Haag and Ritchie. When I returned for dinner, they would both inquire about what I learned that day. I would purposely exaggerate stories about Freud and sex just for entertainment. Once I asked Haag to remove balloons from the dining room table on the grounds that they were phallic. Poor Ritchie blushed with embarrassment, but Haag seemed to enjoy the emotional titillation.

Meanwhile I was busy organizing the religious education classes for public-school students, designing courses for engaged couples, and learning how to deal with the new breed of lay people in Morristown. My biggest challenge was teenagers more interested in studying for good grades than dancing as a reward for attending the CCD classes for public school students. From the beginning I resented that so much money and attention was going to the Catholic school with 300 students, while the Catholic youth who went to the public school received very little attention even though they numbered 450 students.

One day I almost came to blows with the sister principal when she called the Catholic school students "our" kids. I stepped up real close to her, and said, "Sister, they are 'all' our kids." To ensure that others took note of the message, I requested that the registration plates for my new car read "CCD 10." In this way, when others borrowed my car, they were forced to advertise the CCD program. At the same time, I was also busy developing a parish course called the Pre-Cana program to provide engaged couples with a blueprint to form a right conscience, which meant that they could actually use contraceptives to plan their family without sinning in the eyes of God.

While Ritchie and his committee were busy designing a new church for the parish, Ma Haag asked me to head the campaign to raise the remaining money needed to pay for it. I had already worked on one small campaign at St. Agnes Parish and had also learned what techniques worked from professional fundraisers over the years, so I decided to put my fundraising ability to the test by approaching Dorothy, one of the CCD volunteers.

I phoned Dorothy and said, "I need a cup of coffee." She just laughed and said, "I don't believe you would just go out for a cup of coffee in the middle of the day, but come on ahead anyway tomorrow morning." Her street, a private road, had only two mailboxes, one for her in-laws and one for her family. After the cup of coffee, I confessed my ulterior motive and asked Dorothy humorously whether she would consider donating $3,000 for the St. Patrick's statue as a memorial to me, her Irish curate.

She responded as I expected. "You know we are German, although my husband and I were considering that amount." Because Dorothy was one of the parishioners who knew me best, I asked if her in-laws, who owned a successful machine shop, might also give a generous gift. She volunteered to introduce me to them.

At their door, Dorothy's father-in-law greeted me with a warm smile and a firm shake of the hand. His wife, Josephine, a shy woman with a strong German accent, was standing behind him. After the usual pleasantries, I said, "Sir, I don't really know you, but I do know your daughter-in-law. She has been very active in making my ministry to the youth of St. Margaret's Parish a very easy task. This morning I would like to honor her and your family by offering you the sponsorship of the main altar of our new church as a memorial to your loved ones who passed away in Germany."

I could see that he was touched by my genuine sincerity. After a two-minute pause, he asked, "Father Corr, what donation would we be expected to make for this honor?" I replied solemnly, "$15,000 over three years." Josephine nervously started to move towards the kitchen. I called out to her, "Josephine, this is just an offer I want you and your husband to think about." When I rang the door the next morning, he answered and shook my hand firmly. "Congratulations. You are a good salesman. Here is our first check." To top off my morning, Dorothy and her husband pledged $3,000 more. I asked Haag to keep things a secret until the bishop made his remarks on Sunday eve. I wanted to use the success as an example to the committee that keeping our sights high could work. Without too much trouble, we more than reached our goal.

Construction of the new church neared completion. We had convinced the diocesan liturgy committee to accept images of modern-day saints such as Martin Luther King, Jr., Dr. Tom Dooley, and Dag Hammerskjold for the stained-glass windows, which were now installed. The painters were adding the finishing touches to the window frames, and the electricians were installing all of the lights in the sanctuary and nave. Early one Sunday morning, Ma Haag, to his horror, discovered a hole in Martin Luther King, Jr.'s window. Concluding that this was the act of some bigot, he went ballistic at the homily and screamed from the pulpit about the terrible tragedy that had occurred in our parish community. He condemned the perpetrator to hell for all eternity.

Ritchie and I were not totally convinced that this was the end of the story. Our suspicions were validated on Monday morning when the building contractor, who didn't know about the tirade on Sunday, came to apologize because one of his carpenters had accidentally damaged the window when he dropped a hammer. We three priests were too embarrassed to tell the truth to the parishioners. As a result, the story spread far and wide, helped along by the press, who always liked advertising anything that embarrassed the Catholic Church. Six months later, we received a clipping from a London newspaper reporting that racial bigots in Morristown, New Jersey, had thrown a stone through a church window dedicated to the memory of Martin Luther King, Jr.

In spite of Ma Haag's infrequent outbursts of anger, it was great fun living and working with him. Any of us who spent an evening socializing with him could sense not only that he enjoyed being a priest but also that he loved the company of priests. He enjoyed teasing and being teased. If I was working late on a term paper for my pastoral counseling course in my office upstairs, he would bring up a glass of milk and a cookie, saying, "You need energy to finish that paper. I would reply with a slight hint of sarcasm, "Thank you, Monsignor, for your milk of human kindness."

He could persuade other to do things they weren't enthusiastic about doing. On many a Sunday when the priests who weren't on the altar were relaxing in the kitchen over cup of coffee, he would stick his head into the kitchen and say, "Come on guys, let's go out and pat some fannies." Or he might pull us outside the church to greet the faithful coming to mass. Shy Ritchie and I were there one morning when a heavy-set lady approached up the walkway to the church steps. Without the slightest warning, Haag said, "Look at Mary Dee wearing her new girdle before I blessed it." How were we supposed to keep a straight face and greet this sweet lady? She asked, "What's amusing those two vagabonds?" With a straight face, Haag replied, "Who knows, Mrs. Dee? I can never figure out what those two are up to in the morning."

He was a masterful homilist. As senior curate, I struggled to match his skill. Once when I had carefully prepared four typed pages and was disappointed that I hadn't received any positive feedback, he gently advised me that I had delivered my message too stiffly and needed to speak from the heart. At the next mass I raised the sheets above the pulpit and crumpled them into a ball, which I then hurled into the sanctuary. I continued, "I would like to tell you from my heart what is written on those four sheets." The response of the congregation was much more positive than previously. After the mass one of the ushers came up to retrieve the sheets and straightened them as he said with a smile, "Father Finbarr, that was very effective. You should throw the homily pages from the pulpit at all the masses today."

Even though Ma Haag delegated most of the administrative tasks to Ritchie and me, he did more than his share when it came to saying masses and hearing confessions. Because he didn't drive, one of us would drive him weekly to St. Anne's Villa in Convent Station to hear the confessions of the elderly retired sisters. On the way back, when we asked how it went, he would reply, "It is like being stoned to death with popcorn. If you put all their sins together, you wouldn't come up with a decent sin."

One hot evening, he was sitting in the confessional reading his Divine Office with the door open. An older lady approached and asked, "Msgr., are you hearing confessions?" "No," he said, "I am just sitting here waiting for a bus." Very few people took offense at Ma Haag's comments because they had become accustomed to his outrageous sense of humor over the years.

I was in the parish only two months when the parish council members and other leaders, aware of my interest in people having fun together, challenged me with, "Fr. Finbarr, we never have any parish parties or fun at St. Margaret's." I modestly accepted their challenge and suggested that we have a spaghetti dinner on Columbus Day, when we were already drawing a winning ticket for a raffle. Since a majority of parishioners were of Italian descent, it seemed the politically correct thing to have an Italian celebration before we had a big St. Patrick's Day party. Four hundred people came and enjoyed spaghetti and meatballs.

As St. Patrick's Day approached, the neighboring parish heard of our plans and quickly joined in. Volunteers cooked potatoes, corned beef, and cabbage. Others sold the tickets. Our theme was of an Irish cabaret with Irish songs and Irish step dancing. I resurrected the old play *A Breach of Promise in County Cork* from my days in Carlow. My friends from the Good Shepherd Parish in the Bronx heard about our plans and also asked to be invited. Fifty of them, including the "Singing Cop from County Galway" Terry Connaughton, made the trip by bus.

The evening was a huge success. The only minor embarrassment was that three quarters of the way through the dinner, the food committee announced that they had run out of potatoes. I took the blame for that. I should have warned them that all those Irish men from the Bronx would eat at least two potatoes each. In just seven months St. Margaret's became was not just a good parish spiritually. It also became a great parish socially.

"The Party of the Century" at McCulloch Hall in Morristown in 1968 topped all the celebrations at St. Margaret's. Nobody remembers exactly what we were celebrating. The entire hall was decorated everywhere in blue, down to borrowed blue delft and blue flowers.

Told that there would be only thirty minutes rather then the hour scheduled for cocktails, the bar crew doubled each person's drink without telling anyone. The obvious result followed.

Everyone, including our revered pastor Ma Haag, was drunk. Everyone except me, that is. I would probably have been drunk too, except that I was still a total abstainer. I barely reached the head table because several inebriated women lunged at me, to do I don't know what. Once I had managed to seat Ma Haag beside his mom at the head table, I exited through the back door and returned to the rectory. I wasn't scared. I just wanted the crowd to have a chance to eat some of the delicious Italian cuisine and sober up a little. I had discovered early on in the America that there is no worse experience than to be totally sober in a room full of drunks.

When I returned around eight o'clock that evening, no one had missed me. Everyone on the clean-up committee was, to say the least, also incapacitated. Helping take care of the leftovers, I placed a pot of leftover spaghetti sauce on the floor of the chairwoman's car. Unfortunately, her husband, who was three sheets to the wind, stepped into the car and sank his foot, shoe, stocking, and pants six inches into the red sauce. As Mary drove off, she said, "Fr. Finbarr, this is a night we will never forget." Ma Haag looked at me the next morning and said, "Before you came here, we were a quiet parish. You are driving us crazy with all these parties."

Life at St. Margaret's remained hectic and fun, largely due to Ma Haag. He attracted people from far and wide to the parish. He was always willing to say an extra mass or preside at one more funeral liturgy.

He was the most gracious of hosts, welcoming priests from across the diocese and beyond to visit the rectory. His open-door policy also extended to our family and friends. Affirming and warm, Ma Haag inspired us with the freedom and respect he gave us, his young associates. He remains in my memory as one of the most positive priests, and also as one of the most positive people, that I have ever met.

Chapter 8

Fire!!

As Haag, Ritchie, and I sat down in August of 1967 to plan the parish activities for the next school year, we were feeling very good. We had formed a cohesive team. I had many volunteers ready to teach our public school students in the CCD classes. The Sisters of Charity were running the Catholic school without much help needed from us priests, although we stopped in frequently to give moral support. The nuns were feeling happy and appreciated because they had just moved into an elegant new convent that was built under the leadership of Ma Haag. And Haag was very appreciative of Ritchie's and my efforts to make the parish come alive.

On the evening of September 17th, 1967, exhausted from preaching at all the masses that weekend, I went to bed early and fell into a very deep sleep. Suddenly Ritchie dashed though my bedroom to the corridor outside my door. Half awake, I decided that there was a sick call from the hospital or from someone's home and that Ritchie and Haag were taking care of it.

When Ritchie came back a second time, however, and discovered I was still in bed, he yelled, "Get up! Get up! The rectory is on fire, and Haag has fallen down the stairs!"

When I jumped up and opened my door, I saw hell for the first time in a field of flames that was racing up the stairway so close to me that I singed by eyebrows. In my hysteria, and never having been trained as a child what to do in a fire, I signaled that I was going to

89

jump out the bathroom window and land on the cherry tree. My thinking was I would rather die or suffer with a broken backside than die with a burned one.

Ritchie pleaded with me, "Follow me out the window, and we'll sit on the ledge. Someone will hear our cries."

Now it was my turn to help. I knew it would take quite some time for the fire to work its way through my room. I began yelling at the top of my lungs: "Help! Help! FIRE! FIRE!" Finally, a light went on in a bedroom across the way on Columba Street. Someone yelled back, "We'll call the Fire Department." In what seemed like hours, but in fact was only three minutes, the fire trucks came roaring down the street with sirens blowing.

One of the first firemen who climbed the ladder to rescue us was Jewish. To relax us a little he joked, "We cannot blame this on Jewish lightening." The joke was lost on me at the time, although I learned later that it was a somewhat politically incorrect phrase used to describe fires that were started intentionally to get reimbursement from an insurance company.

That morning I experienced indescribable fear and panic. I wasn't at all worried about modesty as I, clinging to my pajama strings, scrambled down the fire ladder. My friends teased me later, saying that I refused to come down the ladder until the press arrived and took my picture. As a matter of fact, a not so complimentary picture on the front page of the local newspaper showed me holding the bottom of my pajamas by the strings.

I can laugh now at some of the dumb things I said, and at the requests I made of the firemen that night.

"Would one of you go back in my office and recover my sermons on the top shelf and please bring me my driver's license?" One of the firemen actually did go back in for the sermons and license. And they covered all my books with tarp so that when they were hosing down the fire they wouldn't ruin them.

Our nuns, who were praying at the convent door down the block, were relieved to see Ritchie and me coming down the street in our pajamas. I am a little embarrassed to report that the sisters invited Ritchie and me to sleep in the convent. With my sick sense of humor, all I could think of was stories we used to tell in the seminary of the tunnels that connected the priests' rectory to the convent. We accepted their offer, but I couldn't sleep. I just lay there thinking, "This is just a nightmare, and I am going to wake up in my own bed, and prepare to say the morning mass as usual." But it wasn't just a nightmare.

By ten o'clock the next morning, news had spread throughout the tri-county diocese that local priests had almost experienced a fiery exit from this world to the next. Our beloved bishop was one of the first to visit. Not interested in the damage to the rectory, he was worried about the well-being and safety of his priests. I told the bishop I would be down in a minute after I had put my pants on.

He had a great sense of humor. He laughed and said, "I will want to know later why you had your pants off in the convent." He reassured us that he would do anything to help us, and that I was to take charge of the parish until Msgr. Haag, whose hands and feet had been badly burned, was released from the hospital.

When the firemen left the next evening, Ritchie and I were invited to have dinner and sleep at the funeral director's home, which happened to be above the funeral parlor. I joked with Ritchie that we were lucky to be upstairs and not down in the morgue. Struggling with the effects of the trauma, Ritchie laughed, but only halfheartedly.

That night I prayed that God would give me the grace and the wisdom to fill Ma Haag's shoes during the couple of months it would take him to recover. Realizing that the show must go on, Richie and I met with some of the parish leaders. All parish programs except for the Catholic school were postponed for a week. With the help of non-union workers, the rectory was not only restored, but we also added a beautiful conference room that also served as the priests' sitting room.

Murphy's Law struck once again when the union workers building the new church learned that we were using non-union workers to rebuild the rectory. The union called a strike on the following Monday morning. I went over to the caravan where the union leader had his office. With all the charm I could muster, I said, "Sir, I am totally wrong. Please accept my sincere apologies. As you can see, I am a young priest with little or no experience of American ways. My dad in Ireland is a hardworking farmer and would be very disappointed in me if he learned that I did anything against the labor movement in America."

He was hesitant to make a response. He knew from the tone of my voice that I was near tears. Finally he said, "Okay, I don't want to embarrass you in front of all your parishioners. I know that if Monsignor Haag was in good health and in charge of the parish this would never have happened." I agreed, "You are absolutely right." The work both on the rectory and on the new church resumed promptly.

Ritchie and I made daily visits to the hospital to help Ma Haag say daily mass and to keep him company. He was becoming depressed, and I sought every opportunity to cheer him up. One day when I was visiting, he needed to urinate, but no nurse was available to assist. Somewhat embarrassed but feeling that I should make myself useful, I offered, "Monsignor, I can help you." He gave that familiar grin and said, "Okay, help me put my penis in the urinal." I did, but not without thinking, "I'll *really* get mileage out of this one when he comes back to the rectory!"

Haag heard about it for the next thirty-five years. When Ritchie and I would take him out each year to celebrate the deliverance from the fire, I would teasingly ask him "Of all the curates you've had over the years, remember which one did the most for you?" He would roar with laughter, saying, "You are right! Only three people other than myself have touched that organ during my life – my mother, Dr. Giordano, and you." Poor Ritchie would blush from ear to ear in hopes that no one seated near us would figure out what we were laughing about.

Once back from the hospital, Ma Haag gradually gained strength. He was motivated to get well as he watched the building of the new church nearing completion. Poor Ritchie, on the other hand, was struggling, and as the time for new assignments came, he asked Haag and me if we would be upset if he asked for a transfer to another parish. We reluctantly accepted his wishes with the provision that he come back to visit us often. We reminded him that the beautiful new church of St. Margaret's of Scotland, soon to be dedicated, was a living tribute to his creativity and ingenuity.

The next concern for Ma Haag and me was whom the bishop would send to replace Ritchie. Fortunately for us there was a good crop of priests being ordained in May 1969. That year's class would be one of the last with more than six candidates. At the ordination Ma Haag and I had good seats in the Cathedral, and we studied each of the seven candidates. All were deacons in their mid-twenties, all except Charles Grieco, who was at least in his early forties. He was obviously a late vocation, having served for years in the army and in the Paramus police. He looked very serious during the whole ceremony, not even cracking a smile when the bishop made a joke during his homily.

As I drove Haag back to Morristown, he was very quiet. I read his mind perfectly. He said what I was thinking. "I hope we don't get stuck with that old guy called Grieco." We were both scared that a holier-than-thou, newly ordained priest would join us and try to change our friendly, slightly off-color culture in the rectory. Our worst fears were confirmed the following Monday morning when the personnel director from the diocese called Haag to ask, "Chris, the bishop would like you to take Fr. Grieco as an assistant."

What could Haag say, except, "Do we have a choice?" The answer was, "This is a very experienced gentleman who has served in the CIA in Europe and been a detective in Paramus for several years. I think he will do well in Morristown. You and Finbarr need to have a priest of Italian extraction to minister to the Italian population."

Charlie arrived with his trunk full of memorabilia from his previous careers. Haag and I were on our best behavior. We avoided sexual jokes and any kind of sexual language. We didn't have to keep our pledge of decency for too long, as Charlie let slip his true colors within two weeks of his arrival. I got up one morning early to say the 6:30 mass. I had a slight sore throat and a cough. As I opened my bedroom door, I could see that Charlie was up already and saying his Divine Office, so I felt comfortable enough to say, "Charlie, would you mind saying the 6:30 mass? I'm not feeling that great." He answered immediately, "Sure. I can do it." Then he proceeded to ask me about my condition. "Finbarr, do you have a tickle in your throat?" I foolishly said, "Slightly." Then he said, "You need to go back to bed and masturbate. Your wet dreams are backing up."

We shared with Charlie our suspicions that the rectory fire of one year ago may have been arson and that there were still acts of vandalism and disruption at the school. We also shared our concern that no one seemed motivated to discover who the perpetrator was. Charlie, a detective by nature, decided to tackle the investigation. He set up a camera facing the auditorium door and wired the camera to a monitor sitting on the TV in the priests' living room. We had to wait only three nights before a not so bright ex-employee came along to the auditorium door with a shovel full of sand. Since I was the person who had fired that employee from his position as janitor at St. Margaret's, I should have felt some guilt for indirectly being the cause of his anger at all of us. Instead I was very angry, but agreed with Ma Haag and Grieco that we should practice what we pray every day at Mass: "Forgive us our trespasses, as we forgive those who trespass against us."

That year turned out to be my last full year at St. Margaret's. I was soon offered a position as Director of the Family Life Bureau of Paterson. I accepted the position on the condition that it be a full-time one. I believed that with all the difficult issues facing the Church - abortion, artificial birth control, the increase in divorce among Catholics - I would be able to do a much better job organizing volunteers and developing programs if I didn't have the added responsibility of daily duties as an associate pastor in a parish.

It was difficult to leave. I felt much loved by the parishioners of St. Margaret's. In three short years, we had all achieved so much together. Not only had we survived a life-threatening fire, restored the rectory, and built an absolutely beautiful church, but we had changed the whole Christian culture of the town by sponsoring the Ecumenical Movement, including double pulpit preaching and living room dialogues throughout Morristown.

My deepest sadness and guilt was leaving Ma Haag, who still suffering from the after effects of the rectory fire. He had been a wonderful boss to me. He had given me almost total freedom to develop social and ecumenical programs that reflected the spirit of the Second Vatican Council, which was in reality the opening the "windows" of the Church to a lot of needed fresh air. He knew of my struggles with celibacy, and was tolerant of my attraction towards beautiful women and of my tendency to be overly affectionate, which he passed off as saying, "That's just Finbarr." He was also concerned that living alone in Paterson without brother priests could be dangerous for me spiritually.

The opportunity was too great to resist. In June of 1969 I said goodbye to Ma Haag, Fr. Charlie, and the parishioners at St. Margaret's to become the first full-time Director of the Family Life Bureau of Paterson.

**Finbarr with friends Dr. Ruth Westheimer
and Sam Levenson**

**Finbarr witnesses the wedding of his sister Marie
to Jack Johnstone**

Chapter 9

A Big Job

One of the greatest thrills a young priest can experience is when his bishop believes in him enough to appoint him to a brand-new position. For several years I had expressed a real interest in the Family Life Movement. Having come from a reasonably stable family, I believed that with the help of others I could contribute strength and care to other families, both functional and dysfunctional.

I was keenly aware that young couples needed more to prepare for a lifelong marriage. With increases in the divorce and teenage pregnancy rates, steps needed to be taken to help individuals and couples cope. Bishop Casey asked me, half humorously, "What are you going to do all day?"

With a budget of $20,000, no bed, no cook or housekeeper, and half a secretary, I set out to change the way 300,000 Catholics in the Paterson diocese looked at marriage, human sexuality, and family life. After a few days of sleeping on the same couch that I also used for counseling, I called the bishop to ask where I was supposed to live, since the home where I had my office wasn't equipped for a residence. He chuckled and said, "I don't believe that I have to worry about you. I don't think you will have any trouble finding a place to sleep."

Slightly amused by his response, I took advantage of his trust and called some friends to tell them of my plight. Before I knew it, I had a bed. Ladies from St.

Agnes' and St. Margaret's also organized a shower for me. Never having attended a shower, I was not at all prepared for the embarrassing moments heaped upon me on the evening scheduled as "A Shower for Fr. Finbarr, new Director of the Family Life Bureau."

At the shower I didn't notice Jane Goretski leave the living room and return shortly thereafter with more packages. She returned wearing a man's nightshirt. The ladies all roared with laughter. When I opened the next two packages, I turned beet red when I saw that Jane had packaged some of her own underwear as proposed gifts. All the ladies had a great night's fun at my expense, and I drove home hoping that the bishop wouldn't hear of my crazy lady friends and how freely they took advantage of my Irish sense of humor. And thanks to Jane Goretski, I have worn a nightshirt instead of pajamas for the thirty years since.

New presidents in the United States usually get a honeymoon of a hundred days in which the leaders of the opposition withhold controversy. My honeymoon in my new job was much shorter lived. Pope Paul VI dropped a spiritual and emotional bombshell one month after my appointment.

The encyclical on birth control, *Humanae Vitae*, was a total surprise for married couples and Catholic priests throughout the world. We in the United States, especially, expected the Holy Father to give the individual Catholic some right in conscience to decide whether he or she was entitled to use artificial contraception in planning their family. However, the Holy Father held a hard line and declared that each and every act of intercourse within marriage must be open to the procreation of children.

At the time of the announcement, I was in Ireland visiting my ailing mother, who was undergoing an operation for cancer. She noticed I was depressed and asked what the matter was. I showed her the heading in the *Irish Press*: POPE FORBIDS ARTIFICIAL BIRTH CONTROL.

She knew that I didn't like the decision. In her inimitable style, she said with a smile, "When the pope speaks, that is the end of the discussion." I wished it were that simple. All hell broke loose among theologians throughout the world.

When I returned to New Jersey a couple of weeks later, I ran into my new and immediate boss, Bishop Casey. He too noticed I was upset. He said, "I need to see you soon regarding the encyclical." I answered, "Sure, Bishop. May I bring a theologian with me? You know what my expertise is in psychology, not theology." He said, "That will not be necessary. Why don't we just meet by ourselves at first."

Was I ever surprised to discover that the bishop didn't keep his word! When I entered his chambers two days later, the charming and conservative vicar general, Msgr. Joseph Brestel, was sitting across the room. Half their age but convinced that I needed to prevent a riot by the parishioners, I started out proactively and slightly aggressively. Looking at Msgr. Brestel, I said, "I didn't expect you to be here, Joe." After an awkward silence, I addressed the bishop with all the Irish warmth and blarney I could muster. "Bishop, I have the highest respect for you and I would never do anything to publicly embarrass you. Some of my fellow priests in the diocese are very upset with the encyclical, and if it wasn't for the respect they have for you, there would be forty of them picketing outside the Chancery Office this morning. We all appreciate the fact that you have not made any public statements to the Catholic press or to the public press about the encyclical, and we recommend that you continue that silence until all the American bishops meet in Minnesota in two months."

Msgr. Brestel was visibly nervous and starting to twitch. I felt that the bishop was still listening intently. I continued, "Until the bishops' meeting, if anybody asks for our response to the encyclical, why don't we say that the people of our diocese will be allowed to follow their conscience until the American bishops meet and make a decision and that if any priest is disrespectful to the Holy Father, he will be reprimanded."

Msgr. Brestel jumped to his feet and protested, "Bishop, you cannot allow that. This is heresy to go against the Holy Father." However, the bishop was swayed by my proposed course of action. I promised to keep our conversation confidential, asked them to do likewise, and headed out the door quickly before old Brestel could change the bishop's mind.

Even though my office was in the city, I avoided the politics of headquarters and didn't visit the bishop's office unless I really had to. I knew I would get along fine as long as I had the blessings and support of Bishop Casey. My next request to him was for permission to attend Columbia University in New York for a doctorate in Family Life Education. Because of his trust in me, the bishop was very honest and said, "Finbarr, you know that many priests who earn doctorates leave the priesthood, but I am not insinuating anything like that about you." I was one happy young man when he gave me the green light to visit Columbia for the initial interview.

Meanwhile, I had started counseling nuns with emotional problems. During my first interview at Columbia University, which was conducted by an attractive blonde woman in a green dress, I was asked, "How do you expect to have enough time to study for a doctorate if you are going to continue all these programs at the Family Life Office, and also counsel religious?" I answered, quite sarcastically, "Maybe I should tell the bishop I am madly in love with one of the nuns and he will release me from counseling nuns."

My interviewer, Eileen, turned beet red. What I didn't learn until the next day was that Eileen was actually Sr. Eileen, a Sister of Charity from the same community where I said daily mass. I called her that same day and apologized for my sarcasm. Imagine my surprise when I was invited a month later to a cocktail party to celebrate Eileen's engagement to Dr. Wolf, one of the professors!

I attended the party and met all kinds of professors and teachers. The most memorable person I met that night was Dr. Ruth Westheimer. She was sitting on a chair, her little legs not long enough for her feet to touch the ground. Having heard of my encounter with Eileen, she called me over and said, "Finbarr, I heard you are a lot of fun. I want to meet you." At that point I had more notoriety than Dr. Ruth. She offered to help me in any of my courses or independent studies. That night was the beginning of our extraordinary and enduring friendship.

For the first time in twenty-eight years of school, I was meeting people outside of my usual Catholic circle and attending a school that was not administered by the Catholic Church. And driving into Manhattan once or twice a week for class was a refreshing break from counseling and preparing Family Life programs.

My next project was to collaborate with the diocesan Catholic School Office on implementing education in human sexuality in Catholic schools. Once again I relied on the political skills inherited from my dad. Fortunately, I didn't need to act alone. I had the support of the other Family Life directors in New Jersey. The Catholic school folks believed that teachers in their schools were more qualified than parents to teach sexual education. We disagreed vehemently, arguing that the parents knew their children best and thus should be the primary teachers in such sensitive matters.

We finally persuaded the New Jersey bishops that our program for parents should come first and then be followed by a holistic program in the Catholic schools that was both appropriate to the age of the students and sensitive to their cultural backgrounds. Now we at Family Life could no longer merely talk the talk. It was time to walk the walk and go on the road to promote the program to Home and School Associations throughout the diocese.

When I described the new project to Mom, she commented, "This is easy. Why would you have trouble sitting down with little kids and telling them about the birds and the bees?" "Mom," I said, "this is much more than about the birds and the bees. We need to help parents teach their children all the aspects of human sexuality in a positive, holistic manner. This is not just about body parts and plumbing."

I was relieved that Mom was in Ireland and not in New Jersey, as she might have joined one of the conservative groups that were springing up to protest that such progressive education in human sexuality only encouraged kids to have sex earlier. Our position was that the children were already way ahead of us.

I was lucky to have several volunteer couples and professional people willing to help. We relied on good films and sensitive language to get our message across. A little Irish humor and my ability to be vulnerable and to admit I didn't know all the answers proved very helpful in forming a bond with the parents. However, the honeymoon was over as soon as the conservative protestors obtained a copy of my schedule.

Dr. Coutinho, one of my top volunteers at the time, accompanied me to one of the meetings. We arrived at the parking lot to find it packed with cars. What we didn't realize until I went into the men's room was that many of the attendees were protestors preparing to heckle us to their utmost. They were actually holding their preliminary meeting in the toilet. One of them was explaining, "I received a phone call alerting me that the pied piper of sex in the diocese, Fr. Corr, is speaking tonight."

You can imagine their reaction when I, standing by the urinal, suddenly said, "Gentlemen, if you wait for a minute, I will join the meeting." They ran out of there as if I had yelled "FIRE!"

As we waited for questions after our presentation, four or five of the protestors started to march abreast from the back of the room towards us. I decided to surprise them again. "Since some people have to go home early, why don't we have our closing prayer?

106

Please stand and join me in saying the Hail Mary." All stood up and said the prayer. I concluded with, "Thank you, ladies and gentlemen, and good night." The protestors were furious and left determined to become more sophisticated in their opposition.

For the next nine months we were constantly heckled, and our adversaries constantly changed their tactics. Once they had a tape recorder hidden and, to entrap me, asked questions such as "Was premarital sex always a mortal sin?" I answered rather casually, "Usually it is. I am certain that there may be a circumstance where it is less culpable than mortal."

That was all they needed. In the next issue of the very conservative paper *The Wanderer*, a lead title article began "IS PREMARITAL SEX A MORTAL SIN? Not so, according to Fr. Finbarr Corr, Director of the Family Life Bureau."

The bishop was tremendously supportive during this period. One letter writer called me a pervert. The bishop laughed and said, "That guy doesn't know anything. You cannot be Irish and be a pervert. They are mutually exclusive!" On that day, he finished the interview by saying, "My job as bishop is easier than yours as director."

Meanwhile, we were also busy organizing "Like to Like" ministries for widows, widowers and divorced Catholics. The chapters of the widows' program held dances every Friday night. I found that I "had" to participate since there were usually not enough men to dance with the abundance of women.

Initiating the ministry to Separated and Divorced Catholics was a different kettle of fish altogether. Many of these members were angry and depressed, and feeling victimized by the spouses who had jilted them. Through local advertising I invited twenty-five divorcees to come to my office in early December.

Twenty-three ladies and two gentlemen arrived to a wine and cheese party with seating around a glowing fire. I greeted them personally at the door, taking each lady's coat and hanging it in the closet. That little act of kindness brought tears to the eyes of a few of the ladies. One lady said, "It has been over ten years since I received such an act of courtesy from any man." They were able to validate each other's feelings and to challenge each other not to become victims of their situation, but to choose to grow emotionally instead.

When it came to expanding the ministry to all the divorced and separated Catholics of the diocese, once again I called on the bishop for help. At a mass for the group where he gave the homily, the bishop surprised us all by apologizing to the three hundred divorcees who attended. He said, "I am sorry that for too long the Church has treated you as outcasts. Most of you here today did not initiate the divorce; you are not guilty of any sin. It is very good news that the ministry sponsored by the Family Life Bureau is now going to be available in all 110 parishes of the diocese." When we priests began giving the kiss of peace, many of the divorcees thanked us with tearful eyes.

With Bishop Casey's support, the Family Life Movement grew by leaps and bounds. We hired our own staff and developed a caring culture for those who came for counseling. We promised, and followed through on our promise, to see every new client who called for help within one week of the initial contact.

Our new public relations person kept our 1,500 volunteers abreast of what we were doing and what our goals and objectives were for the coming year. We opened a second office. Like many other fast-growing non-profit organizations, we began to run out of money. However, within weeks, and with the aid of a friend who was a successful businessman, the Family Life Board of Governors was formed and a fundraising strategy formulated. As they say, the rest was history. The Board ran annual golf tournaments, and held $100 plate dinners with notable speakers like Sam Levenson, Dr. Ruth, and Roland Smith from CBS.

Also, as with any organization within a larger body like the Catholic Church, petty jealousies arose in the face of success. As director I was the natural target of these jealousies. Once, after a meeting in the bishop's office where I had completely lost my temper at two priests seeking to have the Bureau's budget cut, I announced to my staff, "Fellows, you had better pack your bags. I believe I have blown all the fuses at the chancery office."

When the bishop was driven home for lunch that day, Tom, his Dublin-born chauffeur, inquired how the bishop's morning had gone. The bishop replied, "The troops had a pretty intense meeting. Father. Finbarr is a nice guy, but don't get his Irish up." Tom reported back to me that the bishop felt very positive about the Family Life Bureau's achievements, and that he wasn't upset about my blowing my stack.

I had been leading Family Life Movement for ten years and was beginning to run out of energy. I didn't realize that I was becoming addicted to the life style of being on the go for eighty hours a week. I didn't have time for golf or to socialize with my priest friends. I went out for dinner about twice a month, but often for the purpose of recruiting money or time from volunteers. I didn't take time to read my Divine Office, although I said daily mass and helped my brother Jack with weekend masses at his parish. Except for my annual vacations to visit my family in Ireland, I didn't take a full day off for five years. Observing that I had gained weight and had poor color, the bishop ordered me to go to a local doctor for a medical checkup.

The doctor, a Catholic, was already familiar with my schedule. When I entered, he said, "I haven't seen you in years since you were a curate at St. Agnes Parish. I can tell, however, by the number of times that your picture is in *The Beacon* with news of your rallies and jubilees, that you are one busy fellow."

He proceeded to examine me. Suddenly he became very quiet and looked at me with an almost angry face. "You are in trouble, Fr. Finbarr," he said. "You have very high blood pressure, a low heartbeat, and have gained forty pounds. You have all the symptoms for a serious heart attack."

I was stunned and speechless. To add fuel to the fire, he said, "If you continue to work at the same pace and retain the same health conditions, you won't live for more than five years." As he turned away he muttered, "You priests can dish it out, but you are not good at taking directions."

I finally replied, "I get the message. What do you want me to do?" "I want you to join the YMCA tomorrow morning and begin a regular exercise program," he directed.

I went to the gym as instructed and was embarrassed to find that I could only do thirteen sit-ups. When I went back to the doctor a year later, I had a lost a few pounds, gained a lot of muscle, and my blood pressure was 130/80. In the same time, my doctor had gained twenty-five pounds. He smiled when I said, quoting a passage of Scripture, "Physician, heal thyself."

Even though I played racquetball or handball three mornings a week, I continued my hectic work schedule. I had become a workaholic. At a thank-you party for our volunteers, I received a plaque that advised, "Don't hurry, don't worry, and don't forget to smell the flowers." My knee-jerk reaction was, "What does this mean?" The group moaned, saying, "He is much further gone than we realized."

During all this time, I also retained my own clients. Some I saw as individuals or couples, while others who needed more long-term care attended a group session on Saturday mornings. I realized as time passed that group counseling was much more effective than individual or couples therapy. With the help of my supervisor, I had developed a very successful way of creating a climate in the group where every client has an opportunity to grow to emotional good health, although not all of the clients grew without giving me a serious fight.

One divorcee was the mother of four children. She came to one group session quite depressed. The other members and I did our best to raise her spirits. She went home a little better, but obviously not really over it, as she called me an hour later and said, "Father Finbarr, I am calling to say good bye. I have taken twenty-five sleeping pills and I have about fifty more to go."

I tried my utmost to convince her to change her mind, but without much success. I finally said, "I am exhausted. I need to take a nap. I have had an exhausting week. Do you promise not to do anything for the next hour?" She agreed. I actually went to bed and slept for one hour.

Telling the story several years later, I cannot believe that I actually slept, as I had always put the health and safety of my clients before my own needs. When the alarm awakened me, I called to learn that she was the same but at least had lived up to her promise not to take any more pills. I continued my attempts to persuade her to live for her four children. Finally, in desperation, I pleaded with her, "I can see the heading on tomorrow's Sunday paper in Passaic: FR. CORR'S CLIENT SNUFFS HERSELF OUT. That will be the first time that any of my clients committed suicide."

After a moment of silence, she said, "You are right. You are one of the few people who really love me. Why should I hurt you?" I jumped in my car to get her quickly to the hospital to have her stomach pumped. The following Christmas, she sent me a Christmas card with a picture of her four children and the inscription "Thank you, Father Finbarr. Without your intervention these children would not have had a mother for Christmas."

Tommy, another young client in his early twenties, had been cheated out of $6,000 in a get-rich-quick scam and was very deeply depressed. The loss had resurrected memories of many older losses from his childhood. Tommy joined the Saturday group, where he brightened the experience for everyone else. He was amazed at and thankful for his own emotional and social growth during the nine months in the group.

Because Tommy had met his future wife during that year of his rebound, he requested that they have their wedding reception at the Family Life office. He said, "Here is where I have discovered who I am. I want to celebrate this new beginning of my life in this house." Of course, I agreed.

True to an earlier promise I had made to him, I stood on my head at his reception to express my joy at his personal growth. As the reception ended about eleven o'clock that night, Tommy made one more request: "Father Finbarr, would you be upset if we spent our first night together in your home here?" Unfortunately, the only place left for me to sleep was on my office couch directly under my borrowed bedroom. The night didn't help my struggle with celibacy. As my old bed creaked upstairs with their lovemaking, I once again wondered when the pope was going to lift the shackles of mandatory celibacy.

Ten years can be a long time in the life of a priest, but my ten years at the Bureau flew by. A highlight in 1978 was a Family Day rally for 20,000 people at Rutgers Stadium. Twenty years later, I still meet people who thank me for what they learned or gained from their experience with Family Life. Fr. Frank, one of my staff members, probably best summarized things when he commented, "Some priests and lay people may not appreciate the thousands of hours we spent counseling and freeing people to enjoy their lives, but the people we served will remember it forever, and that is something we will have forever that no one can take away."

Chapter 10

Esther Chokes

It is often said that being a priest's sister is a unique vocation. Esther Reining, Fr. Jim Daley's sister, was no exception. She accepted obligations and responsibilities that were not found in the *Baltimore Catechism* or the *Code of Canon Law*. Esther believed that she was appointed by God to watch over her brother. In addition to attending to his physical needs by cooking for him on his days off and taking care of his clothes, she watched over him spiritually. God help any woman in the parish that looked at him romantically! That woman would get such a stare from Esther that the look couldn't be described or imagined.

When Esther was a young adult she met Charlie Reining and fell in love, but Esther's parents forbade the marriage because Charlie was Protestant. Charlie married another woman, who died twenty-five years later. Charlie was at last finally able to marry Esther because her parents were by then deceased and enjoying the Beatific Vision of heaven. Finally, for the next fifteen years, Esther and Charlie were able to enjoy a blissful life together.

Over many years I participated in all of Esther and Charlie's family celebrations and helped them deal with the sadness of sickness, accident, and death. But we also had many good times. I loved it whenever Fr. Jim would say, "We have to stop at Esther's tonight for dinner." Esther and Charlie were deeply insulted if they ever heard that we had dined at a restaurant.

Esther's meals were like exquisite banquets, especially compared to the seminary food.

But Irish luck turned. Jim and Esther's sister Ruth died of cancer. Another sister who was a Dominican nun, Sr. Noeline, also died tragically. Because Esther was a better and safer driver than Charlie, she usually took the wheel when they picked Sr. Noeline up from the convent for a ride in the country. On one of these trips Sr. Noeline died instantly when Esther swerved to avoid a collision and the car overturned. My heart went out to Esther and Fr. Jim, who gave the eulogy at the funeral in spite of his grief. Esther never recovered emotionally from that tragic accident. When Charlie died a few years later, the Dominican Sisters took pity on Esther and invited her to live in their nursing home. Esther was consoled to be adopted by the same religious community to which Sr. Noeline had belonged for forty years.

Through these years, alcohol had taken its toll on Fr. Jim. On Saturday morning, August 20th, 1977, I visited him in the hospital for what would be the last time. I quietly recited the Memorare, a special devotional prayer, and squeezed his hand, with a whisper that he shouldn't be afraid. My former pastor and good friend, one of the most caring people who ever touched my life, died in my arms an hour later.

Once again Esther had to hear that a family member was gone. The deaths in turn of her sisters and brother were real shocks to her, the oldest of the Daly siblings by several years. She was now the last of the clan, but the least qualified emotionally to handle burying her only brother. My colleague Fr. Bill and I promised her that one of us would visit her every week. Because Esther had no living relatives, we decided that her estate might justifiably and eventually go to the Sisters of St. Dominic. With Esther's approval, the Daly family lawyer drew up the will.

On the Wednesday after the document had been prepared, it was my turn to visit Esther. With the unsigned will in hand, I drove to the nursing home. Esther was very happy to sign all of her earthly possessions over to the Dominican Sisters. "May I take you to lunch to celebrate?" I asked. She was thrilled.

The restaurant we chose was packed to the ceiling. The hostess made certain that the priest and the old lady were seated right away. Esther studied the menu carefully. Remembering that she liked to have a cocktail on special occasions, I pointed to the liquor list and queried, "What would you like, Esther?" "I would like a Manhattan and a beef stroganoff," said she, commenting how good Fr. Bill and I were to her. Because I didn't drink any alcohol on the days I had clients, I ordered Esther's Manhattan and a Coca Cola for myself.

Esther gulped down her drink and dug into her beef stroganoff. Halfway through, she suddenly stopped talking. A minute later I looked up to see Esther turning white and then purple. Her body fell forward and her head plopped on the table . . . right into her beef stroganoff!

I started to panic. I thought, "O my God, the ink on the will isn't even dry yet. I'll be accused of killing Esther!" I impulsively put my arms under her waist to lift her face out of her lunch. Finally, she started breathing again. The pressure on her solar plexus had saved her life, and, in my mind, had saved me from prison. To me it was a miracle!

My heart was thumping a mile a minute, and I was beginning to hyperventilate. The waitress was no help. She fainted. I stood up and yelled, "Is there a doctor in the house?" Fortunately, we were close to a hospital, so the emergency squad arrived in no time flat. The ambulance physician handed me Esther's false teeth. "We don't want your friend to choke, Father," says he. I said to myself, "Perhaps if I had asked her to remove her teeth before lunch, she would have ordered soup and I wouldn't be in this mess."

Minutes later, Esther and I were in an ambulance speeding down the highway. Esther came to and murmured, "Fr. Finbarr, I'm sorry to be spoiling your day off." I felt like saying, "No, Esther, it's only Wednesday; sure I do this every Wednesday." Television lights greeted us at the hospital. Roland Smith from CBS, whom I happened to know, asked, "What are you doing here, Father?" I stuttered, "I have an old friend here who choked as we were having lunch."

Roland replied, "It's too bad she's so old. I'm doing a special on children choking. Father, please hurry back; I'm very bored and I need someone to talk to." By this time I was hoping that all of this was really only a bad dream on Tuesday night and that I would wake up from the nightmare to begin Wednesday afresh.

The nurses at the emergency room were most sympathetic to me, a fish-out-of-water priest with all kinds of degrees in psychology but not one ounce of medical training. They applauded my accidental performance of what turned out to be the Heimlich maneuver, a proven technique for saving people who are choking. With Esther in good hands, I relaxed for the first time and began to think of my other responsibilities that day. It was nearly two o'clock in the afternoon and my next appointment at my office was in an hour. Weighing the logistics of getting Esther home but also not missing my appointment, I excused myself to call my secretary at the Family Life office in Paterson.

As I quickly headed to the public phone booth, I experienced another shock that made me certain that I was really going nuts. Even though I was wearing a nice gray priest-like suit with a black vest and my Roman collar, a good-looking nurse in uniform approached and asked me," Did you ever think of marrying?"

"Nurse," I stuttered, "I just had a terrible experience. My old friend almost choked on her beef stroganoff. I am not thinking of sex or marriage just now." She apologized profusely. "I'm sorry. I didn't mean to upset you. You're just kind of cute."

My phone call to my assistant Dee at the Family Life office did not help. Hearing my voice, she immediately asked, "Where are you? We wondered if you had parked your car and were necking with Esther." Why she chose to make that comment on that particular day I'll never know because, back at the office, they all knew it was a real sacrifice for me to give up two hours every other week to visit Esther. I said, "Please don't laugh, Dee. Esther almost died on me at lunch when she choked on her beef stroganoff." Dee smothered a giggle and whispered, "I am very sorry, Father."

I continued, "Please cancel my three o'clock appointment. I am in no shape to counsel anyone. I need help myself." I returned to Esther's side and held her hand as the nurses took her pulse, blood pressure, and an EKG. Esther was worried that she was going to die since the nurses were administering all these tests. I reassured her that she had merely experienced a minor accident due to improper chewing, and that she was going to live for many more years with the sisters.

The sisters relieved me at three o'clock, thanked me for my kindness to Esther, and empathized with me over my nearly tragic day. My next appointment was twenty-five miles away in Sussex County, but my car was parked at the Claremont Diner. I hitched a ride for the fifteen miles to retrieve it and, back at the diner, remembered that I hadn't paid for our lunches. I asked for the waitress who had served us only to learn that she had felt ill and gone home. I wondered to myself, "Did she have some of the beef stroganoff for lunch also?"

The manager approached and complimented me on saving Esther. She added, "I will have your tab ready in a minute." After computing the bill, she sheepishly said, "I have to charge you $9.39; the lady's lunch is free." I laughed to myself, thinking, "Esther ate at least half of hers and coughed it up. I didn't get to eat half of mine." Paying for one full meal seemed fair.

I paid the bill and headed for my car. I hoped that this was the end of the nightmare, but it wasn't. When I unconsciously reached into my pocket for my car keys, instead of finding metal, my fingers closed on Esther's clammy, cold teeth. My next stop was to pick up Sr. Catherine Reilly, a Dominican nun who was scheduled to present a program with me that evening. "Where's Esther?" Sr. Catherine asked as she opened the convent door. Reaching into my pocket, I took out the false teeth. "This is all that's left of her." Familiar with my sick sense of humor, Sr. Catherine ignored my joke and said, "You look terrible. I had better drive this evening."

We had a delightful dinner with a family in the parish, and I felt much improved after a glass of wine. I thought to myself, "I should call the nursing home before it's too late to check on Esther." It was Mother Dorothea who answered the phone. "Good evening, Mother, this is Father Finbarr. I'm checking on Esther," I said.

"Oh, Father, she is fine. I spoke to her a half hour ago. She said she had a wonderful day with you, and enjoyed her lunch very much." Barely smothering a giggle, Mother Dorothea continued, "Esther said that she didn't come straight home from the lunch because the sisters came and took her out to dinner."

"And had the lobster bisque and rice pudding!" I guessed to myself. "Mother Dorothea," I pleaded, "Something terrible happened, and I have her teeth in my pocket to prove it."

When Fr. Bill visited Esther on the following Wednesday, Esther was in good form and made no reference at all to the scare she had given me the Wednesday before. I jokingly said to Bill, "You mean to say you didn't take Esther out to lunch?"

As time went on, Esther's health continued to fail. Just over a year later, Mother Dorothea called. In a somber voice she said, "Fr. Finbarr, I am sorry to tell you Esther died in her sleep last night. We want you and Fr. Bill to concelebrate the funeral liturgy. I am certain that Esther would want you to give the eulogy."

I had no trouble preparing an appropriate homily. I was sure that Esther was already knocking at the

Pearly Gates. Since Bill and I were executors of the will, we felt entitled to give Esther a grand sendoff. We invited all who attended the liturgy at the Dominican chapel in Caldwell to join us for lunch at where else but the Claremont Diner. With input from me, Bill recalled the story of Esther's choking and of how she had dedicated her life to taking care of our mutual friend and her brother Fr. Jim. He finished by saying that he hoped that the vocation of being a priest's sister would continue after Esther.

With fewer priests in the vineyard today, there remains a greater need for priests' sisters - to love us, support us, and keep us out of trouble too.

Chapter 11

Over in Killarney

Throughout my time in America I never lost my love of Ireland and my respect for all that my Irish family, the Irish people, and Irish schools had taught me. I didn't make any effort to lose my strong Irish brogue. I would frequently put my finger to my nose to make a sound as though I were a New Jersey native when people teased me about how I pronounced *Wednesday* (with three syllables) or *Cathedral* (without the "h"). I was satisfied to know that if I spoke more slowly people not only understood my accent but actually found it charming.

Because of my frequent references to my family and my beloved Ireland, listeners often expressed their wishes to visit Ireland and meet my family. They would all ask me, "Does your family have your personality, your charm, and your sense of humor?" I would reply, "Compared to some of my siblings, I am an introvert." I would promise them, "One day I am going to take you to Ireland and to the Corrs."

I finally found the opportunity. I organized a tour to Ireland for which forty-six people quickly signed up. There were bankers, homemakers, carpenters, nuns, lawyers, nurses, and the organist from the cathedral in Paterson. Irish music blasted over the bus's speaker system as we made our way to Kennedy Airport.

As we flew into Shannon Airport the next morning, I encouraged them all to look out the window and see for themselves what had inspired the famous American singer and songwriter Johnny Cash to write "Forty Shades of Green" as his plane was flying over Ireland. The sheep were grazing on the heather atop the mountain, while the cows and calves were munching on the new grass after the farmer had cut the hay. The Aer Lingus pilot announced the forecast: "No rain, sunny, and seventy degrees."

The tour's bus driver Pat and Jim, our courier and guide for the trip, greeted us at the airport with, "How many of you have seen a leprechaun, and would you be interested in visiting a fairy's den?" As we set off for Limerick and the Lakes of Killarney, one old lady muttered behind me on the bus, "Are all the Irish full of blarney? Between the brogue and the jokes it is hard to know when they are telling the truth or just pulling your leg."

Jim had a deep understanding of Irish history and culture and entertained us with a stream of Irish stories and facts about Ireland. Every so often he would break into song and tell a story about one of the famous Irish ballads. One song was "Are You Right There Michael?" The song was a spoof of the West Clare Railroad, which, according to the song, was always an hour or two behind schedule.

The author of the ballad was a popular songwriter named Percy French. Failing to see the humor, the people at the railroad decided to take Mr. French to court in Dublin for defamation of the railroad's good name. On the day of the hearing, all the lawyers and the judge were in place waiting for Mr. Percy, who arrived exactly one hour late. When the judge asked why he was late, he apologized profusely, saying, "I am sorry, your Honor, the train was late." The case was dismissed.

Thoughts of Ireland immediately bring visions of green fields, purple mountains, Galway Bay, and the Lakes of Killarney. As we approached the Lakes along the winding roads, we joined Jim in an Irish medley, ending with one of Bing Crosby's favorites, "How Can You Buy Killarney":

How can you buy all the stars in the sky?
How can you buy two blue Irish eyes?
How can you purchase a fond mother's sigh?
How can you buy Killarney?

Pat and Jim invited us to join them on a private pub tour that night. Jim knew all the pubs and, as with the pied piper of old, led twelve of us through the streets of Killarney in search of what the Irish call the *Craic* (a slang phrase for "fun"). There is no better place to meet the Irish and to experience their wit and charm than over a pint of Guinness in a local pub. The locals only tolerate the tourists from England, but they love the Yanks and enjoy pulling their legs with tall stories of leprechauns, fairies, and banshees, mysterious lights that appeared in bogs and valleys after the death of a local person. Old people in Ireland would casually observe that they knew such and such a person had died because they had seen his banshee on the previous night.

Killarney turned out to be all that it promised. Early the next morning, we climbed into jaunting cars, the one-horse carriages driven by jarveys, local lads with no particular training and jokingly described as either having vaccinated by a Victorola needle or having eaten part of the Blarney Stone. The jarveys told an unending string of tales as they drove us around Killarney's beautiful lakes. We stopped at the local castle for a peek at Irish history. The lucky ones of us continued the night of revelry by going back to the local pub for more Guinness, jigs, and loads of blarney.

I wasn't one of the lucky. One of the older ladies had left her sleeping pills in a bag on the bus and begged me to find the bus driver to retrieve them. Where in God's name was I to find an Irish bus driver at ten o'clock at night in the middle of Killarney? After an hour of searching, as I was passing by one little pub, I thought I heard a familiar voice singing "Danny Boy."

Sure enough, there Pat was, singing his heart out with a few of the locals. Pat wondered why I would be looking for him in a pub at closing time. He smothered a laugh and said, "Father, you really take care of your old ladies, are you sure she is still awake?" Indeed, when with pills in hand I returned to the old lady's room around midnight and peeked in the door, there she was, snoring to her heart's content.

On the way to Dublin we stopped at the Blarney Mills to give our visitors an opportunity to buy Irish sweaters for their family and friends back home. Next door was the Blarney Castle, home of the world famous Blarney Stone. We climbed the rugged stairway and stood in line to be lowered by one of the native sons to kiss the stone that was said to bestow a gift of gab that lasted forever. It came as no surprise to me when a few of our group hollered from the back, "Don't let Father kiss it; he has too much blarney already."

Our next stop was Dublin, the capital of Ireland and one of the oldest cities in the free world. At Trinity College we viewed the *Book of Kells*, a beautiful illustration of the Gospels written about 800 A.D. We saw Dublin Castle, the Abbey Theater, and Grafton Street, one of the greatest shopping streets in the world. Everybody was warned, however, to save energy for the trip to Kells, County Meath, where there would be dinner and a party with the Corr clan.

As we traveled through southern Ireland, I started to prepare everybody for the party with my family. By now my fellow travelers were accustomed to Irish fibs, so I didn't hesitate to tell one more. I said, "My family will entertain you, but they will also expect that each of you will return the favor by singing a song, doing a dance, or giving a recitation. You had better prepare a song or a poem, or we will all be embarrassed on Friday night." What I didn't tell them was that Eilish and Dympna had invited several talented entertainers who were not family members to the party.

The party was to be our last hurrah before we returned to the United States. Because Kells is about forty miles north of Dublin, we gave ourselves ample time in case anybody wanted to stop and see a castle or to stop and see "Mrs. Murphy," as we called going to the toilet. We had plenty of time, so I decided to play a joke on my sister Eilish, at her home in Navan on the way. When our bus pulled into Eilish's driveway, I called out, "Weren't we supposed to stop for cocktails here?" She yelled back, "You haven't changed a bit. I thought a few years in America would have changed you for the better." The Yanks loved to see my sister giving it right back to me.

We found Dympna and several other of the Corrs waiting for us at the Headford Arms Hotel, where special menus for our festive evening read

"WELCOME TO FATHER FINBARR AND HIS YANKEE FRIENDS." Dad, looking fit, was busy welcoming everybody. Mom looked quite frail and chose to sit at the head of the table to greet the visitors. I felt a little sad seeing her there, as I knew that her days were numbered.

Everyone wanted to take a picture of me with Mom and Dad. I wanted the party to last forever. My nieces from Belfast, the stars of the show, were dressed in beautiful costumes decorated with the emblem of their school of dancing. Their dad, my brother Fonsie, was master of ceremonies and welcomed us all to Kells. He told us how excited his daughters were to be invited by Uncle Finbarr to perform for his friends from America, but added that he wouldn't ask Finbarr to sing in return, for that would drive everybody home early.

The meal was a delicious duck a l'orange; the dessert, a gigantic bowl of trifle with angel food cake and brandy. After dinner, the tables were pushed aside to let the dancing and fun begin. I joined the dancers in a little step. For the Yankees' contribution, the cathedral organist from Paterson played some Irish songs and "God Bless America."

Then came a total surprise as Dad and three of his peers, two women and a gentleman in their seventies, danced the traditional dance of Ireland called The Sets. While Beano, one of the local farmers, played the accordion, the four seniors took to the floor and masterfully stepped the intricacies of the old dance known by very few of the younger Irish people.

The party lasted until midnight. Our group made its farewells to all - to the Corr clan and also to those who were pretending to be Corrs. As the bus headed back into the night on the road to Dublin, some kept the party going by singing "It's A Long Way to Tipperary" and other Irish lullabies. Some lauded the Corr clan as jovial and charming, and one added, "Now I know why Father Finbarr is crazy. His family is crazy too."

Along the road to Dublin, some who had more than their share of alcohol called for a Mrs. Murphy stop halfway between Navan and Dublin. Pat didn't see any gas stations on the way, so he was forced to stop along the county road at a spot with some privacy. He apologized to all hands on the bus, but he knew by the screams to "STOP!" that some of the ladies wouldn't make it to Dublin. Those of us who remained on the bus roared with laughter as the others stepped outside, groping their way in the dark. One woman who returned was overheard laughing to her husband and explaining, "It was great to go, but my butt is smarting. I sat down in a bunch of Irish nettles."

As I collected the tip for our tour hosts Pat and Jim, I knew that my American friends would be generous, but I didn't expect them to be as generous as they were. The amount was the biggest tip that Pat and Jim had ever received. On the other hand, to the Americans, the tip was a very small price to pay for the fun and adventure of visiting Ireland and meeting the Corrs, a milestone that all agreed they would never forget.

Chapter 12

Meeting Dr. Ruth

As I was completing my master's program in pastoral counseling in May 1969, my supervisor encouraged me to go on for a doctorate at Columbia University in New York. After having driven fifty-five miles each way for three years, commuting half the distance into New York City sounded easy. I found a doctoral program in family life education at Teachers College of Columbia University that seemed the appropriate choice for my purposes. Once I had reassured the bishop of my intention to stay in the priesthood, he gave me permission to register.

Before long I had become something of a conversation piece in the halls of Columbia. There I felt comfortable for the first time in public for people to call me Finbarr rather than the usual Father Finbarr. I realized that my time there could be a real growth experience that would expand my horizons. For the first time, at thirty-four years of age, I was attending a non-religious school as not only an active Catholic but also a priest.

Dr. Ruth Westheimer, then an associate professor at Columbia, had already heard of the new student with the cute Irish brogue. More than the brogue, I'm certain that she reached out to me because she was a very insightful and caring person who realized that, in spite of my outward show of bravado, I would find the transition to Colombia a serious personal challenge. My recollection of her from our first meeting is of a diminutive lady with a strong German accent and magnetic personality.

The few words we exchanged on that first encounter were the beginning of a thirty-year friendship that sustained each of us through many transitions in our lives. For myself, there were many days during the next five years that I wanted to drop out of the doctoral program altogether, but Ruth wouldn't let me. She would always say, "Finbarr, you will never know. One day you may really need a doctorate." How prophetic those words were!

I signed up for the course "Various Alternate Family Lifestyles" led by Professor Paul Byers, who at one time had traveled to visit strange tribes around the world as the assistant and photographer for the well-known anthropologist Margaret Meade. Introducing the course, Mr. Byers explained that he would be inviting prostitutes, wife swappers, and commune people so that we could learn how other people lived their lives. Angrily, I shot to my feet. "Dr. Byers (I was being sarcastic as I knew he didn't have his doctorate yet), would you consider a father and mother of ten children as a possible lifestyle in America?"

Some students giggled; others looked startled, thinking that I was some right-wing conservative ready to deck the professor. Later, some confessed to having suspected that I was an Irish cop because of my brogue and my big feet. In any case, I created a hostile atmosphere in the class that Mr. Byers quickly diffused by saying, "You are absolutely correct, sir. Would you mind taking the class that day?" I answered sharply, "Yes sir, I will."

In my previous twenty-five years I had always attended Catholic schools. At Columbia I met fallen-away Catholics disgusted with the Church's overly controlling attitude on birth control and abortion. Pro-Choice people were sometimes openly hostile to me. Once, when the discussion focused on the pros and cons of abortion, I took a middle-of-the-road position. I suggested that people should not use abortion as a family planning technique, that contraception was a better moral decision. One listener, a woman who worked in a New York abortion clinic, and who happened to be lying on the floor of the classroom at that moment, had had enough of my preaching and retorted, "Finbarr, you are nothing but a male chauvinist pig priest." My Irish up, but with all the charm and solemnity of voice I could muster, I replied, "Only the pigs on our farm in Ireland portray the same poor deportment as you, and they lie and grunt from the mud, just like you." Even the Pro-Choice people in the class loved the way I answered her. And that was the last time she tried to attack me.

As the semester progressed, Professor Byers and I agreed that the class I organized would be a panel of three Catholic couples, who would discuss how they had grown in their marriages while at the same time respecting the tenets of the Catholic Church. When the day of the presentation arrived, several students, even some of those who were my friends, decided to skip the class. As a student from South Africa said, "Finbarr, we love you dearly, but talking about Catholic marriages for three hours has to be one of the most boring afternoons imaginable."

To almost everyone's surprise, those three hours became the talk of the cafeteria for the next week. I had invited one very articulate couple from the World Wide Marriage Encounter Movement to speak about how their daily writing and reflections on feelings had substantially improved their communication. The other two couples were from the Christian Family Movement, where, along with eight other couples, they had met weekly for prayer and discussion for ten years.

The openness and vulnerability of these couples provoked powerful thoughts in the listeners. The panel shared how they formed their own consciences on issues of birth control, ending up at times with actions that appeared diametrically opposed to the pope's encyclical. They even shared that one meeting they all threw their car keys into the center of the room and discussed with one another what it would be like if either party was free to sleep with the person whose keys they picked from the floor blind-folded. The traditional Catholic students in class were shocked to hear these ideas discussed by Catholic couples. The married couples reassured them that they didn't swap spouses, as they came to the conclusion that they had each shared something more valuable with their spouse than mere physical sexual pleasure over the twelve years.

Halfway through the class I started to worry that my fellow students were unusually quiet, very different behavior than when the prostitute and the wife swappers had presented. When I inquired why my colleagues were not challenging the panelists, they responded that they were very moved by the presentation and by the couples' openness, and that they were thoroughly enjoying the session. One fellow student came to me privately after class and said, "Finbarr, I am ashamed to say that I gave up on the Catholic Church in 1959 and I regret it now. The changes brought on by the Second Vatican Council seem to have given more freedom to its members on how they relate to the Church and its precepts." That day and from the whole course, I learned that liberal people are not always as closed as I sometimes judged them to be. Paul Byers even invited the Catholic couples to participate in the following semester's repeat of the course.

My narrow legalistic eyes had been opened to broaden my perspective and objectivity. I began to feel that I was living in two different worlds. I had the experience of continuing my priestly duties of saying mass daily for the nuns and helping as a weekend assistant at a New Jersey parish. In the latter role I felt privileged and up on a pedestal, while in class at Columbia, I was just another lay student. The only time I was treated differently was when one of our professors invited all of the students except me to his home for a party at which marijuana was going to be offered. When I heard about it afterwards, I wasn't upset, as I believed that I wasn't ready to be in a place where illegal drugs were being served. What I worried more about resisting was the temptation to go to bed with a female student where there was mutual attraction. But with the help of my spiritual director, I avoided any serious sexual complications.

The time I spent at Columbia changed my life view, but it almost killed me as well. The challenge of keeping my job at the diocese, attending classes, and doing papers added up to eighty-four hours per week. I realized that I needed bring some balance back into my life. I took some time off for golf and for socializing with friends, at least during the weekends. I exercised at least three times per week. My spiritual advisor helped me regain a personal relationship with Jesus. Developing a habit of centering prayer several times a week made me feel that not only had God created me but also that He had a plan to watch over me for the rest of my life. Placing myself in His presence and listening to Him gave me a sense of inner peace that I hadn't experienced in years.

I was getting good grades at Columbia without compromising my obligations to the Family Life Movement. With additional funds being raised by the Family Life Board of Governors, I was able to hire more staff to help with the lectures and public relations work. I used some of the Family Life programs as subjects for independent studies at Columbia. During this time Dr. Ruth helped me on a continuing basis.

I was thus very surprised when I received a call from her in spring of 1975 to ask if I would become her supervisor as she switched careers for the third time to become a therapist in the area of marriage and sexuality. For a full year she drove out to my office in Paterson every Saturday morning. She would counsel a few couples from nine to twelve, and I would give her supervision for a half hour. She loved to talk, so my first task was to force her to actively listen to her clients. I must not hint in any way that I was in any way responsible for her enormous success. Her genius in developing a worldwide consciousness of sexual literacy was solely due to her hard work and to her ability to communicate sexual information in a humorous and sensitive manner.

In time, I was given more opportunities at Columbia to do research in my field and to share it with my classmates. One research course involved a study of how organizations function. The literature revealed that inequalities arose when some sections of an organization obtained so much control that it inhibited the growth of the whole organization. I naturally chose the Roman Catholic Church as my subject. Previous studies had revealed how the pope and the bishops had kept priests subject to them by certain sanctions, and how the same priests had a kept the lay people in the Church subject to them. When my paper was complete, I presented it to twenty colleagues. They deeply understood the core issues in spite of their richly diverse cultures and religious affiliations. One Episcopalian colleague from South Africa commented, "Finbarr, you are bright enough to be a bishop, but they will never risk choosing you." Everybody howled with laughter.

After much thought and research, I decided to use my doctoral dissertation to integrate the subjects of the priesthood and pre-marriage programs. The thesis referenced "the possible relationships between the background variables of priests and the manner in which they counsel engaged couples." Father Andrew Greeley, the priest sociologist from the Archdiocese of Chicago, was most supportive when I told him about my topic. He had just completed a very large study of the American Priesthood at the request of the American bishops. When I asked him if I could adopt some of his questions for my research questionnaire, he said, "I usually say no, but how could I refuse a fellow Irishman with a strong brogue. You remind me so much of my relatives in the west of Ireland." Dr. Ruth volunteered to be on my team along with two other professors from the Home and Family Life Department.

The population I chose for my research was a random sampling of all the priests of New Jersey. Because I was chairman of the New Jersey conference of Family Life directors for that year, I had the opportunity to make my request before all five bishops and four auxiliaries. Two of the bishops were totally in my corner. Two of the others argued that I couldn't include questions about priests' sexual attitudes and relationships with authority in my questionnaire.

One bishop felt quite threatened and asked under what authority could Columbia University or I evaluate the behavior and spirituality of priests. Another came to my defense again and said, "Bishops, shouldn't we be encouraging this young man to do research on something valuable to the Church and his ministry, rather than studying two flies going up a wall." When one opposing bishop saw the questions, he called all the other bishops and forced them to join him in aborting my project. This was more than ironic because those same questions to which he objected were taken from the questionnaire used by Andrew Greeley and approved by the United States bishops just two years earlier for the national study.

The final resolution was that I would send my questionnaire to all the priests of our diocese of Paterson, which would achieve the same purpose for my sample. Questions regarding attitudes towards sex and towards authority were omitted. The research was a huge success, with eighty-one percent of the priests responding. I was amazed to substantiate that as many as twelve different aspects of priests' backgrounds could potentially influence their interactions with engaged couples.

On the day of my final defense, I was confident but very nervous. Dr. Ruth kept me calm as I prepared for the emotionally charged moment where I would defend my two years of research and results before a panel of five qualified professionals. There was only one awkward moment when a panel member asked,

"Mr. Corr, what do you intend to do with the results of your research now that you are finished?" I blurted out, "I plan to use it to renew our pre-marriage programs in New Jersey." Suddenly remembering that each new finding needs to be retested before implementation, I quickly retracted and said, "Doctor, before I use it I plan to have another colleague look at it and see if my results stand up to more research." The answer accepted, I was asked to leave the room so that the panel could decide my fate.

The next twenty minutes were the longest I have ever experienced in my life. Suddenly the door opened and my little friend Ruth announced in her own inimitable accent, "Doctor Corr, will you please come in?" The "Doctor" was the signal that I had passed. The day of graduation arrived. Shirley Kudock, a good friend, accompanied me to the graduation ceremony since most of my family was in Ireland. Shirley reminded me, with a smile, "Now you can take time to smell the flowers."

That was June 15th, 1975. I was very grateful to God for Ruth Westheimer, as she was the inspiration I needed to help me reach that important milestone and fuller perspective in my life.

Chapter 13

Christmas in Belfast

As Mom's health failed, Dad nursed her with great patience and love in her final days. When she died in 1971, we tried to persuade Dad to move in with my older sister Eilish, but he insisted that he would be just fine taking care of his dog and himself. I resolved that he should not spend the Christmas holidays without some member of the family with him. I had no official parish responsibilities that year, so I departed for Ireland a few days before Christmas. Dad has retired after sixty hard years of framing. Unaccustomed to being emotional, he was waiting for me with tears and open arms at Dublin airport.

I had forgotten how cold and damp the winters were in Ireland. Dad was so accustomed to the weather that he was quite comfortable just wearing a light jacket. I needed a heavy winter coat, scarf, and gloves. He reassured me that he had put a big fire in the stove at home to make things warm for this poor lad spoiled by central heating in America. In spite of the cold weather, the fields were still green as we drove down the winding roads to County Meath, where Dad now lived in a little house in the village of Loughan. Many of the houses and little country stores were decorated with the traditional holly and Christmas wreaths. Dad's big collie dog greeted us as we drove up.

As I entered the kitchen, I was shocked to see a huge plant covering seventy percent of the kitchen table. I said, trying to hide a smile, "Dad, your plant is beautiful." He answered, almost tearfully, "This was your mother's favorite flower. I keep watering it because it reminds me of her and her love of flowers."

The next two days were difficult for me. This was my first time at home since Mom had died. All I kept thinking about were our great joyful Christmases as kids in Legaginney. I thought of Mom and Mary Farrelly plucking the geese and burning the small pinfeathers off over the turf fire. I could still smell the smoky flavor of goose ready to be stuffed and cooked for Christmas dinner. Mom's Christmas pudding, with its variety of fruit ingredients and flavored with brandy, would be appropriately aged and tasty. My brothers Colm and Fonsie and I were sent to the woods of Drumcarbin to pick two kinds of holly, the green with red berries and the all-white holly. There is no better place in the world, or time in the world, than celebrating Christmas as a child in Ireland.

But now I was chatting with Dad and sitting by the fire trying to keep warm. I was a little anxious about going up to bed and sleeping on cold damp sheets. Dad, one step ahead of me, had resurrected Mom's old hot water bottle and had it piping hot in the bed two hours before bedtime. Dad was all smiles looking into the fire and happy to have his priest son home from America for Christmas. I was sitting there imagining at any moment that I would hear my mom Nell walk down the stairs from their bedroom. I heard a creek upstairs and looked over at Dad. He had heard nothing. He sat, perfectly relaxed, gazing at the blazing fire. A warm silence permeated the kitchen.

"Dad, what are we doing for Christmas dinner?" I asked. He answered with a grin, "I have a surprise for you. I wasn't going to tell you until tomorrow. Your brother Fonsie has insisted that we spend Christmas with them in Belfast." Having read all about the *Troubles,* as the conflicts in Ireland were called by the locals, I asked Dad, "Is it safe to cross the border on Christmas Eve?" Dad answered quite firmly, "I was never afraid of the English soldiers, and I am not going to start being afraid now."

After mass the next morning, we stopped at Mom's grave near the little church at Carnaross. Dad had bought a beautiful headstone with her name inscribed and with a place left for his own. He smiled and said, "It won't be long until I am lying there beside her." We said the Lord's Prayer for Mom, and went on to the village post office where Dad introduced me to the local postmistress: "This is my son, Father Finbarr, home from America to spend Christmas with me." Before I could ask for an airmail stamp, she asked, "Father, did you ever meet my cousin Louise? She lives on 14th Avenue in Detroit, Michigan?" I tried not to smile. "I am sorry, ma'am, I didn't. Detroit is a long way from New Jersey." She smiled from ear to ear as she gave me the stamp, saying, "America must be a very big country."

Dad surprised me with a delicious breakfast of eggs, bacon, and toast. He had never cooked while Mom was alive. Perhaps necessity is the mother of invention after all. As we prepared to head to Belfast I sensed that Dad wanted to drive, as he had for many years. Once when his own doctor had refused to give him a letter certifying he could renew his driver's license, Dad changed doctors. The new doctor asked, "How old are you, Mr. Corr?" Already past seventy, Dad answered "Sixty-five" without batting an eyelid. The doctor just smiled and signed the letter.

Along our way, towns were filled with last minute Christmas shoppers, and the air rang with joyful music. We approached the border stop that separated northern and southern Ireland. Perhaps because of the holiday, the English soldiers carrying rifles with bayonets were pleasant and didn't search our car. One of them asked politely why we were going north. Dad replied, "To visit my son for Christmas." The soldier wished us a Happy Christmas and waved us on.

In my wildest dreams I never imagined that I would spend Christmas in Belfast with the family. But here I was at Fonsie's home. Having greatly missed seeing nieces and nephews as they were growing up, I listened intently as they told me what they expected Santa Claus to bring them for Christmas. Breege, a favorite niece, was teasing her sister Caroline that she would find coal in her stocking because she had been naughty during the past year. Caroline, wanting to continue the myth of Santa for her two younger sisters, pretended to be upset.

While Dad and I were enjoying nice warm meal and the customary pot of tea, I began to think about the focal point of the Christmas celebration, the liturgy in honor of the birth of the baby Jesus. The Irish Church was known for its celebration of Christmas. Local choirs hymns prepared hymns for weeks before the season arrived. I remembered that, for me as a child, Christmas was more a spiritual holiday rather than a time of tinsel, toys, and expensive gifts. To add to my joy, Fonsie announced that he had arranged for me to celebrate midnight mass with the local pastor.

Arriving at the church, I quickly learned that the pastor wanted me to be the sole celebrant for the whole church full of his flock at midnight mass. I was overwhelmed and protested, "But Father, I have no homily prepared." He just smiled and said, "I don't believe that will be any trouble for an American priest with all your experience." I didn't have time to get nervous. Fonsie patted me on the shoulder and said, "Go for it. You can do it." He left me to sit with his family and Dad in the front pew.

A beautiful choir greeted me with "Come All Ye Faithful" as I processed behind the altar servers to the main altar. A whisper went through the congregation: "We have a guest priest tonight." I remembered that as kids back in Potahee we always loved having a guest priest at our church. I ad libbed a few words of welcome and introduced myself as the brother of Fonsie Corr, who was well known to the congregation. Christine, his six-year old, excitedly called out for everybody to hear, "Hello, Uncle Finbarr." Christine's mother, Mary, blushed. I answered, "Hi, Christine," and she cuddled beside her dad.

As the mass began, I sensed that everybody in the congregation was listening intently to each word I said, and to the words of the Sacred Scripture being read by the lector. Everybody rose as I began to read the Gospel story about how the shepherds on the hills of Bethlehem were startled in the middle of the night when angels suddenly appeared in the sky to announce that Jesus, the Prince of Peace, the Savior of the World, was born. The angels announced further that the shepherds could find Him in a stable with Mary and Joseph, where He was wrapped in swaddling clothes and lying in a manger.

As I started the homily, the words began to flow. I observed the many families sitting before me and began to think of the many families who had lost some of their members because of the violence between the British soldiers and the Irish Republican Army. I pictured some of their fathers and brothers at that very moment in Long Kesh prison in Belfast. I gently invited the people to come with me to Bethlehem. I said, "Let's join the shepherds. Bring all your pain and hurt, all your needs, and place them in the manger with Jesus." I didn't want to mention the Troubles from the altar, as the Irish understandably didn't like foreigners coming over and telling them what was wrong with their country. I asked them that when they are making their Christmas offerings to include their worries and anxieties in the collection basket so that I could offer them up with the bread and wine to Jesus, our Lord and Savior. I ended my homily on a very personal note and a personal request. I told them how special the night was for me, to offer Christmas midnight mass with my dad and Fonsie's family, and with all of them.

I had never had this experience before. My personal request was that, besides sharing gifts and Christmas greetings with their family and friends, I wanted them to think of someone in a particularly painful way. I paused and asked, "What would it be like to visit that family? What would you say or do to bring the peace of Christmas to a family in so much pain? What would you do?" I looked out for a minute, in silence, at all of them, and then slowly walked back to the president's chair.

As I offered the gifts of bread and wine, the choir sang "Holy Night" and several other beautiful Christmas hymns. The pastor helped distribute Holy Communion, the bread of life, to all the faithful. The procession to the altar continued for several minutes, as everybody wanted to receive the Eucharist on the birthday of Jesus who gave us this gift of becoming man. As the mass ended, the pastor rose to thank me and got a big laugh from the congregation when he asked, "What did you think of his homily?" When they all applauded loudly, he announced, "Father did that without any preparation. You can imagine what good homilies he gives back in America when he has lots of time to prepare."

This was becoming one of the most wonderful Christmases I had experienced in many years. The only really important person missing that night was my mom, but I was comforted to know that she was looking down from heaven on all of us. I thought all of the surprises were over for the night but it wasn't to be so. Fonsie announced, "There is a man in the rear of the church who insists on meeting you."

Mr. Paul McConnell, a little man with a very firm handshake, was one of Fonsie's bank customers. He was looking up at me with reverential eyes as he spoke: "God bless you, Father. That sermon tonight was one of the most beautiful sermons I have ever heard. I was wondering, Father, if you would mind doing something that you asked all of us to do tonight. Our family is in terrible pain. Our little nine-year old daughter, Deirdre, has cerebral palsy. She is a lovely little girl, but has never spoken. I believe that you are a very holy and blessed man, and have the power to heal our daughter. Would you come this afternoon to our home and give her your blessing?"

This was much worse than being asked to give a homily unprepared. The sins of my whole life suddenly appeared before me. I never thought of myself as a holy man, much less a healer. Mr. McConnell was obviously a very sincere man of simple and strong faith, and I didn't want to disappoint him. For once in my life, I was stuck for an answer. My own faith and my belief in miracles were being called into question. Back in my office in Paterson, I would sometimes say, "Miracles happen in my office but I don't cause them. God works through me in bringing healing to people, but you have to let Him in to allow the change to happen."

I didn't want to give this little homily to Mr. McConnell. He was looking for me to visit his family on Christmas Day. Fonsie, sensing my discomfort, grabbed Mr. McConnell's hand and suggested, "Instead of us coming to your home today, why don't you and your wife bring Deirdre over tomorrow night and have some tea and Christmas cake." Mr. McConnell accepted the invitation and I felt rescued, for the moment at least. We bade Happy Christmas to the pastor and went out into the chilly air.

Fonsie wanted Dad and me to see the lights of Belfast, so he took us up to the top of a hill in Carryduff, the little suburb where he lived. Looking up at the sky, we could see the new moon and hundreds of stars that make up the Milky Way. We also saw the seven stars in the shape of a plough that Dad had pointed out to us as children. Since the sky was particularly clear that night, we were able to see the Morning Star, the brightest star of all. I couldn't help wondering whether this was the same bright star that had guided the wise men from the East to the manger in Bethlehem. Overcome with the sense of peace of the sky above and the radiance of the lights of Belfast below, I paused for a moment and prayed over the troubled city that Jesus the Prince of Peace would melt the hearts of both the Republicans and Unionists, and bring Ireland, North and South, to a final and everlasting peace.

I fell asleep that night having forgotten all about the McConnell family and their extraordinary request. But, sure enough, at ten minutes past six the next evening, the doorbell rang and in came Mr. and Mrs. McConnell with Deirdre. Mrs. McConnell, a cute little lady with a sprig of holly in her lapel, was very chatty like her husband. She was also a woman of great faith and couldn't wait to tell all of us in the room how excited they had been coming home from midnight mass. She quoted relevant parts of the homily, especially the part where I asked people to visit a troubled family this Christmas. She also stated her belief that I could heal Deirdre.

To change the topic, I asked why Deirdre was wearing a helmet. Her mother answered politely, "To prevent her from hurting her head, as she frequently faints if she hears a sudden sound." Deirdre joined Breege on the living room floor and started playing with the toys like any little girl. My sister-in-law served all of us tea and cake, while I was getting more nervous by the minute, wondering why Jesus would ever listen to the prayers of a sinful priest. Since the family seemed to be relaxed now, I decided that a smoke of my pipe would help me relax and possibly prevent me from having a nervous breakdown myself. I carefully cleaned my pipe and filled it to the brim with sweet smelling tobacco.

Without thinking of Deirdre, I opened my lighter and flicked the wheel that rubs against the flint. As usual, the spark ignited the wick soaked in lighter fluid. The lid of the lighter snapped shut, causing an unusually sharp clang. Oh my God! That did it.

Deirdre, who had been walking around, crashed to the floor and remained motionless. Now I was really frightened. Instead of curing their daughter, I thought I had killed her, so young a child. Mr. McConnell noticed my embarrassment immediately and said, "Father, don't worry. This happens all the time when any person makes a little sound. She will be okay in a minute." Sure enough, Deirdre woke up and started playing again with Breege on the floor.

"Enough is enough," I thought. "This family is not going to leave without the "holy" priest from America praying over their daughter." I got down on my knees near both of the little girls, and I just let the prayer come as spontaneously as my homily did at midnight mass. "Loving Jesus, today we celebrate your birthday throughout the world. We ask your special blessing on Deirdre, Breege, and their parents. Please, Jesus, let these children show to their parents how much they appreciate their love and the care that has been bestowed upon them all these years. Amen." I never mentioned the words *healing* and *cure*. They just wouldn't come out, yet, the McConnells were thrilled and left with Deirdre after thanking all of us profusely. Neither Fonsie nor my Dad questioned why I had chosen that prayer. I am glad they didn't, as I didn't know myself.

I slept soundly that night after an eventful Christmas Day in Belfast. The first sound I heard was the phone ringing at about eight o'clock the next morning. I heard Fonsie say, "Good morning, Paul. Aren't you up early?" Then he said excitedly, "Is that right?" There was a long pause, then, "Sure I will tell Father Finbarr. He is still asleep I believe."

147

Fonsie couldn't wait. He burst into my room and said, "When Deirdre woke up this morning, she spoke for the first time ever and said 'Thank you, Mama.'" I firmly believe that Fonsie thought I had performed a miracle. I realize I have many faults, but I am not delusional. If it had been a miracle that God performed through me, then Deirdre would have continued talking afterwards, just as the blind man in the Gospel continued to see after Jesus cured his blindness. Deirdre did not continue talking and, as a matter of fact, she never spoke again before she died four years later.

There is a wonderful tradition in Ireland that takes place on St. Stephen's Day, the day after Christmas. In celebration of the feast, people dress in costume with masks and go from home to home collecting pennies, mostly to bury the wren. The wren, according to folklore, revealed the Deacon Stephen's whereabouts to his captors by flying out of the bush where Stephen was hiding.

Fonsie and Mary's girls were too small to go out themselves, but they enjoyed meeting the wren boys who knocked on their door. Fonsie, Dad and I shared stories of the wren boys who came to visit Legaginney when we were little. We knew most of the visiting wren boys in spite of their disguise. One lad we enjoyed in particular as children was Father McEntee's servant boy who came dressed in Father McEntee's old pajamas. He brought his accordion along with him and asked his fellow wren boys to dance a gig in the family's kitchen before he collected his few pennies.

Not wanting to overstay our welcome, Dad and I left for his house two days later. We all agreed that had been quite a memorable and beautiful Christmas.

As Dad sadly said goodbye to me at Dublin airport, I invited him to come visit me in the United States. He smiled and said, "I may surprise you all." Within six months Dad did actually book a flight to New Jersey, but then cancelled it on the advice of his doctor. I never did have the opportunity to hear an opinion about anything directly from him – whether the topic was the most recent activity of the IRA or my latest achievement. But, as always was the case since my youth, I continued to hear from his neighbors that he was very proud of me.

Chapter 14

The Pastor

Six years after Mom passed away, my sister Eilish called me home. Dad was dying of heart failure. He was still conscious when I arrived from the airport. He smiled and gave me a sign that he knew he was dying. I took out my beads and started the rosary, Dad's favorite prayer. His lips moved ever so slightly as we said the Our Fathers and Hail Marys. As we said the final prayer, he seemed to slip into a coma. I held his hands in mine. About twenty minutes later, his breathing became labored. Wanting to observe the old Irish custom of holding a lit blessed candle in the dying person's hand to ward off evil spirits, the nurse reached for the blessed candle. Minutes later, we listened to him take his last breath. In my twenty-eight years in active ministry, Dad's was the only death I ever witnessed other than Fr. Jim's.

Several local priests celebrated the funeral with my brother Jack and me. I was the designated eulogist, as I had been for Mom's funeral in 1971. I kept my feelings under control until we were processing to the cemetery in Carnaross to lay Dad to rest beside Mom. I suddenly found myself crying like a baby. They were both now gone, and, with their deaths, Ireland would no longer be home for me.

My second father, my spiritual advisor and sponsor Bishop Casey, died that same year. After his death I began to realize that my days at the Family Life Bureau were numbered. Bishop Casey's successor

150

believed in putting the Church's energy and focus into spiritual and educational programs at the parish level. Even though it was only a matter of time, I continued to work hard in my last two years at the Bureau. The Family Life Board of Governors grew and flourished. After a successful Family Day rally for 5,000 people, our Bureau joined other Family Life Bureaus in the state to hold a statewide Family Day rally for 18,000 people at the Rutgers University Stadium in 1978. I invited parishioners at local parishes to join the parish Family Life committees, and with help increased the number of volunteers to 1,500.

The great strength and the extent of the volunteers' unselfishness and dedication constantly surprised me. One volunteer gave up a good job as a company secretary to direct Birthright, a new program to help young ladies, married or single, deal with the problem of an unplanned pregnancy. Some of the volunteers could never say no.

One couple finally decided to take a weekend to go to the shore, away from their children and from their avocation – volunteering for Family Life. The husband begged his wife, "Please don't tell Father Finbarr what we are doing or where we are going." Their weekend went well until Sunday morning when they turned the television on to check what time it was. On screen, as large as life, was Father Finbarr saying, "The Lord be with you." They both doubled over with laughter, exclaiming, "You can't escape him. He even follows you into motels!"

My Irish priest colleagues helped keep my spirits up with their constant pranks. Very late one night, after an evening full of engagements in another parish, I tiptoed back into the rectory where I was a guest, trying not to wake my hosts. I wondered why so few lights were on. I didn't have a flashlight, but remembered that I was to sleep in the visitor's room just inside the hallway. I was feeling my way in the dark and doing quite well until I pushed open the bedroom door. Suddenly, a pot and pan fell on my head with a bang that could be heard throughout the whole house. Momentarily frightened, I heard a laugh from the top of the stairs where a voice from the dark said, "That will teach you not to stay out late on Saturday nights."

One day, as we were nearing the tenth anniversary of Family Life, my new bishop phoned to talk to me. "How are you feeling today, Finbarr?" Without waiting for a reply, he went straight to the point. "Finbarr, I have been thinking about who the next pastor of St. Vincent Martyr Parish in Madison should be. I would be very pleased if you would consider accepting the position." I impulsively blurted back, "Bishop, you know that Madison is full of Italians. I don't know if my Irish brogue would be a good fit there." The bishop answered, with a very deliberate tone, "Finbarr, I believe you are exactly the person they need right now."

It was always difficult for me to leave an assignment, and this time was no different. I considered whether prayer would help me decide. Since my days as an altar boy in St. Michael's Potahee, I had enjoyed a good prayer life. My prayers, unfortunately, were mostly prayers of petition that asked God to change His mind, as it were! I was often very frustrated because I felt that my prayers were not answered much of the time. Gradually, I realized that God had more things to worry about than whether I received a good grade in an exam.

152

I now saw my past approach to prayer as very foolish. Centering prayer, to which I had recently been introduced, taught me that God has a plan for each of us and that the objective of prayer should be to learn how to accept that loving plan. The results were much more positive. I became more centered as a person, and was actually amused sometimes at what the plan seemed to be. I also became much less frustrated when things didn't go exactly as I wanted them to.

With these reflections and experiences in mind, I responded to the bishop, "May I have the weekend to think about it? I will call you back on Monday." What I didn't mention to him was that my discernment of God's will was going to take place in Las Vegas, Nevada. Invited there by good friends who realized that I was tired, I prayed my Divine Office and used the meditative phrase "Not my will be done, Lord, but Your will" as I sat in my bathing suit at an outdoor pool. In spite of the distraction of pretty ladies flitting around in bikinis, the Spirit seemed to be working.

As promised, I called the bishop on Monday morning and announced, "Bishop, if you wish me to become pastor of St. Vincent's, I will accept the nomination." His reply was a shock to me. He seemed to be changing his mind when he responded, in a very different tone than in his previous call, "Finbarr, don't do it just because I want you to. I want you to do it for yourself."

I thought to myself "Son of a gun, he has invited somebody else!" The game switched from a gracious, complimentary invitation to a competition between me and some other invitee. Without sounding alarmed, I responded, "Okay, Bishop. I'll throw my hat in the ring." He replied, "Good for you, Finbarr. The diocesan personnel board will call you for an interview."

When I attended the priests' silver and gold jubilee celebration the next day, nine fellow priests greeted me and congratulated me for my appointment as pastor of St. Vincent's. I felt like a proper idiot. I finally admitted, "It hasn't been decided yet, but I've thrown my hat in the ring."

I also learned that my friend Father Patch, who had served as an associate for many years at St. Vincent's, was angry with me. For sentimental reasons, he had wanted to finish his career as pastor of the "Rose City" of Madison but, as I later learned, had been discouraged from applying once I became the lead candidate.

Soon the appointment was official. Before I started, I made a commitment to myself to change my style of leadership. I no longer wanted to be the sole decision maker responsible for every detail. I wanted to share leadership with my associate pastors at St. Vincent's. My predecessor, a very dominating leader, was somewhat uncomfortably surprised when I asked that the two associate pastors be present for the transition interview. He also didn't appreciate my being late for the 10 A.M. meeting on his day off. Nor was he excited about my Irish sense of humor when I asked if he would lift me over the threshold. I learned during the meeting that the parish was well organized structurally, but with a very traditional, authoritarian model of leadership. I said to myself, "That's going to change!"

The day of my move arrived. As I drove into the rectory yard at Madison that Saturday evening, the gothic church with its many gargoyles was magnificent and imposing in the late afternoon sun. Standing in the back of the church before the five o'clock mass, I met John, a wonderful, gracious man of Italian descent who had been an usher there for many years. I asked, "John, what should I say to introduce myself to the congregation tonight?" He answered with a smile. "Father, be yourself and you will do fine."

Everybody at the five o'clock mass knew John. When I explained that skipping the homily had been his idea, they all howled with laughter. I continued, "I am a family man, and I'm grieving because I'm leaving the Family Life Movement. Before I accepted this assignment, I called one of your previous associate pastors, a man you know who is very direct and honest.

When I asked him for his advice, he said, 'Take it, Finbarr, you're leaving one family and joining another. St. Vincent's is really a family.' I concluded my brief remarks with, "What you see is what you get. I'm sure we will get along just fine."

As I was unpacking and getting settled in my new quarters, I felt a tremendous pain in my chest. My immediate thought was, "Oh my God, I'm dying!" Not wanting to frighten my two new associates, I hurried to the home of a former client who was a registered nurse and asked her to take my blood pressure. It was perfectly normal. She kindly explained, "Father, this is normal stress that people often go through when they're changing jobs." The pains in my chest soon subsided, and I felt perfectly fine by the time that my first day as a pastor ended.

I had learned in my studies of systems organization at Columbia University that a priest doesn't decide to take over the leadership of a parish. It is the congregation that decides to let the priest be their leader. This process often takes at least eighteen months. Fortunately, at St. Vincent's I had two good associates to help things along.

The first priest, Fr. Ed, loved people and spoke Italian fluently. He was loved by the people, but it was obvious to me very early on that his ministry and personality had been stifled by the previous style of leadership in the parish. Fr. Ed didn't know what to make of me or of my sense of humor and what he perceived to be a very laid-back attitude. Later he confessed to me that he had stereotyped all Irish priests as prisoners of alcohol and the racetrack.

The second associate, Fr. Joe, was a respected preacher and teacher. He already knew me as a caring person who was sensitive to fellow priests as brothers, so he was less confused than Fr. Ed. I asked each of them what their interest and gifts were and how they could best assume leadership in the parish. Because Fr. Joe was a good liturgist, I asked him to organize everything that happened in church, which included scheduling who said which masses, training the altar servers, acting as liaison to the church choir, and many other tasks. I added, "Joe, this is your area to run, just tell me what mass I am saying." To enable his leadership, I only requested that, if he desired to make any change in the church, he review it with me first and then explain to the congregation why he thought the change was needed.

Fr. Ed shared with us how much he enjoyed speaking Italian and that he would be willing to act as liaison to the Italian-speaking community. He also volunteered to be moderator of several parish organizations, including the Rosary Society and St. Gerard's Society. I agreed to be a liaison to St. Vincent Martyr School until the time when the principal became part of the pastoral team.

We also agreed to weekly rotation of responsibility for visiting the sick in the hospital. Both Joe and Ed shared my conviction that the educational programs for public school students needed to be to be brought up to the same level as the Catholic school. We agreed to meet weekly as a team and to help each other with homilies by reading the Scriptures for the following Sunday at those meetings.

St. Vincent's parishioners were accustomed to good liturgies, and I tried hard not to disappoint them. I engaged the congregation by using a conversational tone and included many personal stories, along with the Gospel messages. Parishioners would say, "You were talking to me today, Father." I found it very easy to preach at St. Vincent's, especially with the welcoming climate set by several wonderful choirs.

Unfortunately, I was of no use to the choir because I couldn't carry a tune, but I did have its sympathy and support whenever I did my best to intone the Our Father. Whenever I wanted to be humorous about a second collection, I would say, "If you are not already motivated by this fine cause, think of it as a donation to pay for the pastor's singing lessons."

During this period I was determined not to become a workaholic again. I worked hard to keep a balance in my life. I made sure that each day included prayer, exercise, intellectual stimulation, and good emotional relationships along with its eight to ten hours of work.

Thursday was my day off. I enjoyed my monthly trips to the Bethlehem Center in Chester, New Jersey, for an overnight meeting with a priests' support group.

I was also determined to make the rectory a real home where people laughed and felt free to tease one another. The parish secretaries, who had their offices on the first floor near the dining room, would often join the priests for a cup of coffee in the dining room. We quickly became a family and I encouraged Ed and Joe to have their priest friends and family visit us as frequently as they wished. Initially, our wonderful cook Theresa found it difficult to cope with the rectory's open-door policy, but she soon learned to cook extra since we never knew how many would be stopping in for lunch or dinner.

Having lived without a cook for ten years at the Family Life Bureau, I was unaccustomed to good meals. McDonalds had often been my source of nourishment. Since Theresa could match any chef in Morris County in providing first class cuisine, I found it nearly impossible to pass up any of her cooking. I gained ten pounds in just the first six weeks. Naturally, Theresa was as disappointed as I when I had to inform her that the days of elegant menus and constant desserts were over for me.

Meanwhile I spent a lot of time getting to know the parishioners and letting them get to know the real me. They learned to tease me about my accent, and I teased them back with, "Why do you think the bishop sent a psychologist to be your pastor? Does he think you're all crazy?" I visited the school regularly and got to know the teachers and the children. The little ones in the first and second grade would run up to me in the classroom to give me a hug when I would jokingly say, "Father Finbarr doesn't feel good today. He needs a hug or two."

As a therapist I was aware that young children could easily become attached to a priest and would want to visit him at the rectory for an affirmation or a hug. Because of my experience of counseling religious and families, I was very much aware of the disorder of pedophilia. While I was also aware that I didn't have this malady, I was careful never to give adults or children any cause for suspicion. If a little girl or boy came to the rectory and asked to see Father Finbarr, I would ask the secretary if she or he was alone. If the answer was yes, I would come down from my office and visit the child in the presence of the parish secretaries. If there were two or more children, I would allow them to visit me in my office.

A particular little red-haired girl named Sarah had a congenital hip problem and walked with a limp. My heart went out to her, and I gave her an extra hug and asked her what she wanted to be when she grew up. She explained, almost in tears, "Father Corr, I would love to be a dancer." Heartbroken for her, I replied, "Sarah, if you have faith and trust in God, you will dance one day if it is His will. I will pray with you and you know that nothing is impossible with God." Years later I almost fainted when I learned from a parishioner that Sara had been dancing for one year with the Richmond Ballet. You have to believe!

One Ash Wednesday morning I was walking out of the church. My new black breviary was carefully tucked in my left hand. The children, escorted by the teachers, were approaching from the school for the 8:30 mass. I watched the children as protectively as a real father would. Suddenly I noticed a patch of black ice directly in the path of cars coming down the little driveway hill to the church parking. Gripped with fear, I worried that if any driver applied his car brakes too quickly, the car might slide down the hill straight into the group of children.

At that instant I saw a young lady driving her Honda and approaching much too fast. Waving my breviary wildly to slow her down, I leaned out over the mound of snow in front of me. Truly stubborn, the young lady failed to slow down and kept coming apace. I impulsively tried to jump over the mound with my long cassock, and, of course, landed off-balance on the slick ice. My legs flew out from under me and up in the air. To save my new breviary, I held my left hand up and landed on my wrist, which, as you might expect, took the impact of the fall.

While I was still sprawled on the driveway, the stubborn young lady drove past me slowly, parked her car, and walked straight into the church with the children. She completely ignored her poor pastor writhing in pain on the ice. My hand was going one way, and my wrist another. My new breviary, incidentally, was fine and without a scratch. I went to the sacristy to tell Fr. Joe, who was expecting me to help him distribute ashes. I held up my poor wrist, expecting him to say, "Oh my God, you broke your wrist!" Instead he only muttered, "You are of no use to me. Get someone else to help me give out the ashes."

Chapter 15

The Parish Comes Alive

As I began my new job at St. Vincent's, I promised myself that I would not make any significant changes or even talk about change for at least the first half-year. I kept that promise for four months. While attending the parish council meetings, I sensed that the parish council members were waiting for me to tell them what we would do. They didn't realize that they were going to be the leaders along with me and the other members of the pastoral team. They did perceive that Fr. Ed and Fr. Joe were happier as priests and that the pastor himself was joyful and welcoming to all. Now my goal was to discern with them where the spirit of God was going to lead our faith community and to involve them in mapping out the details of the path.

Over time our pastoral team was expanded to include the school principal, the director of religious education, and the youth minister. With humor and dialogue, we developed a trust in each other that far exceeded our expectations. We could argue and debate at our meetings on the second floor of the rectory, and then come down to lunch in the dining room and immediately be teasing each other and telling jokes in a good-natured manner.

Because of my past experiences with the pastors I had served, I was especially determined that when I became a pastor I would try to create a real home for my associates. I made Frs. Ed and Joe feel

161

comfortable in inviting their family and priest friends for meals at the rectory. Every so often we would take a break from the parish, go to the retreat center, and share a half-day of prayer before our parish planning session. We would have an annual outing to New York for a play or dinner in Greenwich Village. One year on my birthday the team took me to see an Irish play entitled *Mass Appeal*. Its two characters were an Irish pastor fond of his whiskey, and an effeminate seminarian. We priests saw ourselves in much of the dialogue. The actor playing the pastor didn't look much like me, but the rest of the team thought his Irish brogue sounded one hundred percent like mine, which made the play very enjoyable for them.

When I asked Fr. Joe if he thought it necessary to bring an Irish actor all the way from Ireland to play the part of a drunken pastor, he looked at Fr. Ed mischievously and complained, "Ed, we wasted a whole afternoon and $5 bringing him here. He doesn't get it!" Once more I recognized that taking jokes from the team was the fair tradeoff for dishing them out myself. I soon decided that living with two younger priests who had a good sense of humor and who weren't afraid to carry their part of the responsibility of ministering to 1,800 families was a lot more fulfilling than living alone in a big house in Paterson.

After several months, we were ready to include the lay leaders. One of them, a social worker and married priest name Gerry Gannon, developed a survey that was both entertaining and informative. We invited 150 lay people representing all of the parish organizations to a covered dish supper. With plenty of comedy, Gerry warmed participants up by saying, "We're not too sure how this new pastoral team is doing. They hold secret meetings and don't give us any minutes."

After a pause he continued more seriously, saying, "St. Vincent's Parish belongs to all of us. I think it's only fair that we should have a say in how it is run and what the goals and objectives are. The pastoral team has asked me to assess tonight where we are as a community of faith before we make plans to move forward. Tonight we want you to critique five areas of parish life: the liturgies, the preaching, the administration, the social ministry, and the social life of the parish. We want you to be totally honest in your answers, and not to be afraid to be direct. I will provide 'protective armor' for the team, so please don't just give answers that you think they want to hear."

That comment drew laughs from everybody. Continuing, Gerry explained that Father Finbarr, the new pastor, talked a lot about St. Vincent Martyr parish as being a family, and said, "I know personally that he means it. This is the first of many family meetings we'll have as we move forward together."

Most of the feedback was very positive. In some cases there were negative comments, which the three priests accepted graciously and sometimes with humor. One group reported that they sometimes had difficulty understanding the preacher in church. Everybody laughed as I responded, "Obviously, they are referring to Father Ed or Father Joe, since I speak perfect King's English."

We published the survey results in the parish bulletin. The openness became contagious. We heard from people of all walks of life in the parish - single adults, widows and widowers, divorcees – all of them asking for help and making suggestions because they all wanted to be part of the "new" parish. I asked the parish council to define the parish by creating a mission statement. We adopted their proposal that "the mission of St. Vincent Martyr Parish is to heal and renew the parish family according to God's plan."

Parishioners grew increasingly enthusiastic as this concept was incorporated into homilies and talks. Several new organizations took root that same year: Ministry to Youth, the 30+ Club for Single Adults, Social Ministry to the Poor, Parish Hospitality, the Young Couples Club, and the Pre-Cana Team.

One request from the original speak-up was, "Why don't they publish how much the Sunday collections are? Does the parish have a budget? How much money do we need to collect weekly to meet our budget?" Talking about money was not one of my favorite things. People could easily tell by my body language and stuttering voice that I wasn't at all comfortable with the topic. However, bolstered by ideas about Christian stewardship, the pastoral team and the trustees accepted the concept of persuading people to donate their time and talent to the parish. A subsequent fundraising campaign was authorized to solicit their treasure.

The trustees were anxious. The cost of the new ministries was increasing, but the collections remained at just $5,000 per Sunday. We estimated that twice the amount was needed to cover all the expressed needs. I asked the trustees for just one year's grace before we launched an Increased Giving Campaign. Although the pastoral team and trustees had faith in my leadership, some of the financial folks on the parish council were not as trusting.

One gentleman proposed that the parish borrow $10,000 each from several wealthy parishioners, making it a tax-deductible donation for them and giving them interest on their loan. The proposal was rejected by the rest of us, but not without the gentleman who proposed it hurling an insult at me: "Father Finbarr, you may be a great shepherd, but as an administrator you are a zero." Sorely tempted to reply, I practiced my anger management skills instead.

As we made plans for 1980, I decided that since I had been denied the opportunity to celebrate the year of the family on the diocesan level, we could use the theme "Celebrate Family," created by the United States Catholic Conference of Bishops, to develop the family spirit of St. Vincent's. The diversity of the parish's nationalities gave us good opportunity. First, we organized a committee to celebrate Italian, the most dominant culture in the parish.

The all-weekend celebration began with mass in Italian and a homily outlining Italy's contribution to the Catholic Church. An exhibit of Italian art and pictures of famous Italian sculpture filled the auditorium, which was transformed into an Italian villa. The celebration climaxed with a wonderful Italian dinner of veal scaloppini and all of us, including the Irish pastor, dressed in traditional Italian garb. The *vino rosso* (red wine) flowed and we danced the tarantella until the band wished us all *Buona Notte* (Good Night).

Those who missed the big dance wanted to make certain that they didn't miss the next cultural celebration, which they guessed would be an Irish party around St. Patrick's Day. Now that the parishioners had their first Irish-born pastor in one hundred years, they were expecting a really special celebration as the day drew near

Ireland's contribution to the world at large was both spiritual and cultural in nature. Hardly a country or a little island in the world hasn't been visited by an Irish missionary. Also, Ireland had made tremendous contributions in the fields of drama and literature, with poems by Yeats, novels by James Joyce, and plays by J.M. Singe and Brendan Behan all quoted and enjoyed around the English-speaking world. Irish music was the foundation of Bluegrass music in the United States.

The challenge facing the Irish celebration committee was to take all of the above and condense it into a parish celebration. Celebrating a mass in Gaelic and preaching about how Irish priests and nuns helped spread Catholicism around the world was easy. For the art, we obtained pictures of the *Book of Kells*, Celtic crosses, Irish woolen sweaters, and several pieces of Waterford crystal.

Tickets for the dinner of corned beef and cabbage and Irish beer went like hot cross buns. Many who were unable to obtain tickets for the dinner came to the evening mass at five o'clock to hear the Irish liturgy. The choir included Celtic music and ended with the traditional Irish Blessing:

> *May the road rise up to meet you,*
> *May the wind be always at your back,*
> *May the sun shine warm upon your face,*
> *And the rains fall soft upon your fields,*
> *And until we meet again,*
> *May God hold you in the palm of His hand.*

The air was electric as we all proceeded to the school auditorium for the dinner, concert, and dancing to follow. I was all gussied up in my Irish Aran sweater and my best dancing shoes. The auditorium, decorated with harps, shamrocks, and bouquets of flowers at every table, was breathtaking.

While the DePortere boys were doing their jigs and reels, one of the boys faked an injury. Their gregarious mom came and grabbed me saying, "Father Finbarr, you cannot let the boys down. They need you to make up for the Four Hand Reel. Patrick is hurt." What I didn't realize until later was that the whole plot had been set up for days. Being a good sport, and with a little bit of Irish whiskey that killed any inhibitions I had left at that point, I took to the floor. The whole place went wild and started clapping. The choir especially loved it, as they remembered me saying jokingly many times, "I am a dancer, not a singer." As judged by the applause and the lack of boos, I did well. At nine o'clock it was time for the Biddy Early Band from County Clare to take over and provide the dance music both for the Irish and for those who wanted to be Irish for the night. Any woman who could dance that night wanted to dance with Father Finbarr. The play *A Breach of Promise in County Cork* ended the evening.

Our parish census also revealed that we had at least sixty-five families of German descent, forty Polish families, and one Chinese family. The Germans, not wanting to be upstaged by the Italians and the Irish, prepared a fine liturgy that included a traditional oompapa band and a presentation on German Catholicism. The committee borrowed art from the German Consulate in New York. Similar to our other cultural celebrations, we dressed up in German costumes, drank German beer, and ate our fill of sauerbraten and red cabbage.

Polish weekend, which followed six months later, highlighted the fact that Poland had produced the first non-Italian pope, John Paul II. I contributed to the collection of art and memorabilia by adding a picture of the Holy Father with me, taken outside his private chapel during my previous sabbatical in Rome. We danced the polka, ate plenty of kielbasa, and toasted each other with Polish wine. I bought a Nehru jacket for Indian weekend. For the Chinese celebration, the Chinese priest added a special ceremony involving prayers for the dead, which no other nationality duplicated. We each included our own deceased relatives in the ritual.

Energized by the new spirit, people who had never before been active in the parish found themselves drawn to participate. The spiritual and educational programs flourished in parallel with the social and community growth. A new director of the religious education program developed the regular sacramental program for grammar school students, and also worked with Father Joe to develop an adult education program and the Rite of Christian Initiation for Adults to educate converts.

We worried that the teenagers were being sadly neglected. We had the usual Catholic Youth Organization that sponsored basketball games, dances, and bus trips to the New Jersey shore, but little was done to assist in their religious formation or spiritual development. When the issue of our need for a full-time youth minister arose, I decided to run an experiment. I volunteered to give a three-week workshop on Sunday evenings for all high school students on the very juicy subject of "Teenagers and their Sexuality."

For the first session, thirty teenagers turned up. I knew enough about teenagers from my courses in psychology to know that I had to get their attention in the first three minutes or otherwise I would lose them for the full hour, if not forever. I walked to the blackboard and wrote in large letters '"SEX!!!" and asked casually, "What do you know about this?" Snickers trickled around the room.

One brash young gentleman decided to challenge me: "What do you know about sex? You are a priest." I was ready for him. I said, "Stand up, Michael." When he did, I sat down in his seat and said, "You seem to know more than me. Why don't you lead the discussion tonight?" Quite embarrassed, he replied, "Okay, Father. You win."

I continued, "Michael is partly right. None of us, especially me, knows everything about the beautiful gift of human sexuality that God has given to us. We don't understand what the drive is in each of us that craves intimacy with the opposite sex." There was absolute silence in the room. My vulnerable statement "none of us, especially me" had captured their attention. I added, "We men are strange animals. We are attracted to girls and we want not just an emotional relationship with these beautiful creatures, but if they would cooperate, we would want a physical union as well." Michael's eyes were ready to pop out of his head.

Then I asked, "Why is it that women are so attracted to us guys, craving our attention, our romantic gestures, our presence, and our security?" The girls loved it. I ended by saying, "My role here this evening is not to preach at you, but to facilitate a discussion on these sensitive topics and to help you manage these wonderful feelings in a positive way."

They had expected me to lecture them on topics such as mortal sin, premarital sex, and impure thoughts, but they left the session totally shocked and pleasantly surprised, I'm sure. The next day the news soon circulated to their Catholic classmates at Madison High. One of the teachers overheard one of them say, "The new pastor at St. Vincent's is an older guy, but he's cool." We had initially planned on space for forty people, but quickly had to adapt because sixty teenagers turned up at the next meeting. The Sunday after that it was one hundred teenagers wanting to participate in the "Odyssey on Human Sexuality" featuring Father Finbarr.

As in the movie *The Field of Dreams*, if you build it, they will come. As Fr. Joe had recommended, I hired Livvy Dineen, a qualified youth minister, with Fr. Joe as moderator. Livvy created a great team of youth advisors and developed a youth ministry second to none in New Jersey. Three hundred teenagers participated in weekend retreats called Search and prepared for the sacrament of confirmation not only by learning theology but also by reaching out to the neighborhood through charitable works for the elderly and poor of Madison.

As with any growing organization, Murphy's Law also often prevails there also. Josephine, a quiet and patient secretary who was in charge of organizing funerals and coordinating details for the parish cemetery, made the mistake of not telling me something very important – that a body was lost in the cemetery.

I first got wind of the problem when I received a call from the state attorney general informing me that a family of former parishioners had issued a complaint. Their dad's body, buried in St. Vincent's cemetery twelve years ago, was missing. The family owned a double plot and had buried dad in a blue suit and wearing his glasses. When their mom passed on, they naturally requested that the second plot be opened so that their parents could be together for all eternity. The problem was that when our very faithful gravedigger Michael opened the grave, the family's dad and his coffin were missing. Michael was persistent and didn't rest until he found the coffin four graves over.

To make matters worse, the funeral director broke the law by opening the coffin without the proper legal permission. Sure enough, when he lifted the lid, there was the deceased himself in his blue suit and his spectacles still on. He was looking none the worse for having been in the wrong grave for twelve years. The next day, as the family was burying mom and replanting dad in the proper grave, I offered to demonstrate my apology for the error by saying the graveside prayers. The family refused to accept my offer, saying they had their own priest and didn't want to trust a priest from St. Vincent's.

Later we discovered that Ernie, the previous gravedigger and an alcoholic, had been in the practice of agreeing to "rearrange" the cemetery in exchange for a six-pack of beer. Regarding the gentleman in the blue suit, when Ernie had once been told that the man was buried in the wrong grave, he didn't move the body. The ground was frozen and covered with snow, so he simply moved the headstone four graves over.

I recovered from my embarrassment pretty quickly since, fortunately for me, the original burial had taken place long before I took over the watch as pastor. Josephine, however, took the situation badly because she had been secretary of the cemetery at the time when Ernie worked there. Anxious to avoid further mistakes, she began asking me questions every day that ordinarily she would have handled herself.

Once she asked me what should she do about a family who had buried their dad in the cemetery but refused to pay the fee for opening the grave. If Michael or any of the other secretaries was listening, I would pretend to be very upset and say, "Josephine, if they don't pay within a month, up he comes." Being pastor of a parish that had a cemetery was a unique experience for me. It probably was the source of my wish that when I die my body be cremated and the ashes spread over some golf course in Ireland.

The increased enthusiasm in the parish and an energetic Increased Giving campaign helped us increase the Sunday collections by forty percent in just one month. The weekly collections actually increased from $5,000 in 1979 to over $14,000 by 1986. After a short rest, we began to address the challenge of the decreasing enrollment at St. Vincent Martyr School. During our administration, we had made every effort to integrate the school into the total parish mission. It wasn't an easy task. Many parishioners complained that the subsidy paid from the general parish funds was excessive ($165,000 annually). Considering that only one third of the children of grammar school age from the parish attended the school, I couldn't argue with their complaint. Enrollment was dropping drastically because many parents were taking their children out of the school for the seventh and eighth grades with the excuse that Catholic schools could not compete with the educational opportunities available in the public school system.

During my first few years as pastor, I had become very close to many of the teachers and students at the school and made it a point not to interfere its administration. I visited the school regularly, not to supervise but to offer my support to a very dedicated staff of teachers, many of who were teaching there long before I came. I became increasingly impressed with their dedication in spite of the fact that their salaries were much lower than those of teachers in the public school system.

To address the school problem, I returned to an old technique that had worked over my past twenty-five years in the priesthood. I called a few experts in the field to join a committee that included a parent representative, the dynamic school principal Ms. Bennett, and me. Mr. Jack Callan, a college professor and a very objective educator, agreed to head the group. The committee addressed curriculum issues, marketing, public relations, and how to increase enrollment. From the group's very inception, Ms. Bennett and the teachers were very appreciative and excited. For some time they had been feeling that the school was falling behind as the other parish ministries flourished. I had gained their confidence over the years because they recognized that my love for the children was genuine. Fortunately for me, I had their trust, which became essential when the committee determined that some tough decisions were necessary if the school was to survive in the long run. We had, already closed the eighth grade temporarily because the experts had advised us that there weren't enough students for socialization (twelve students minimum).

To assist with the marketing, during Catholic Schools Week we invited parents to give witness talks from the pulpit outlining what a Catholic education meant for their children. We held information nights and open houses. We invited grandparents to come to school for a day. The children cooked a turkey for the luncheon. The first graders loved seeing me dressed up in an apron with a chef's hat, and each wanted to be in a photo with me and the turkey. I loved visiting them, especially those in the lower grades. I would drive the first grade teacher crazy when I entered the classroom and said, "Father Finbarr doesn't feel good today; he needs some hugs to make him feel better."

By 1987, I realized that I might not be around St. Vincent's for the next ten years, so I took one more step to guarantee the survival of the school. Again with the help of some of the lay people, the St. Vincent Martyr School Foundation was founded to raise at least one million dollars from wills and donations. The intent was that the interest from the endowment would subsidize the school. The project was enjoying a brilliant start when I resigned as pastor in 1988.

St. Vincent Martyr Parish was and is a special place where people of many cultures pray, work, learn, and recreate together. Like any human family, it is not perfect. It has many positive qualities - a love of good liturgies, a caring attitude towards the poor, a nurturing concern for their priests, and a desire to create a climate where visitors are welcome. If any reader wants to choose a parish where their children can grow to full maturity as Christian gentlemen and women, my advice is "choose St. Vincent's."

Chapter 16

The Silver Jubilee

After five years the people of St. Vincent's had embraced the team approach to ministry and no longer came to me to answer all their questions. There were some personnel changes. Father Ed, frequently sick due to New Jersey's unpredictable weather, moved to California. With my encouragement, Father Joe returned to school to obtain a master's degree in social work so that he could pursue his interest in counseling.

As pastor, I led the pastoral team, helped organize the Pre-Cana group, planned the ethnic celebrations, and carried my share of masses and of visiting the sick. However, because the pastoral team and an excellent parish staff took care of the other usual parish needs and emergencies, I was free to give workshops and travel to out-of-state seminars. I also had time to finish my first book, *From the Wedding to the Marriage*, a professional guide for priests and ministers on how to counsel engaged couples.

But I didn't let my professional obligations consume me as they had when I headed the Family Life Bureau. I took time out daily for centering prayer and reading the Divine Office. Once a month at Bethlehem Center, I met with *Jesus Caritas,* a group of twelve other priests who were like brothers, for an overnight of prayer, life sharing, and fellowship. I was comforted to realize that some of these priests were also struggling with the loneliness of the priesthood. Like me, they tried to reconcile the tensions of ministering to a people whose principles were totally democratic, but yet within a Church administration that was highly monarchical.

I shared with my support group how lonely and angry I felt at losing the fellow priest who had been my close friend and confidant in America for thirteen years, Fr. Denis Haughney. Denis had died suddenly of a heart attack at the age of only fifty-five. Preparing for his funeral mass, I struggled with anger and sadness as I selected the readings and prepared a homily to reflect his positive, cheerful ministry. Tears blotted my writing pad. At the service, I reflected on the Gospel story of the holy women coming to the tomb to anoint the body of Jesus. I invited the mourners, who included Denis' sixty-one cousins, to join me in rolling back the stone of grief that prevented us from seeing Denis in his new state, enjoying the Beatific Vision in heaven. I shared the stories of my adventures with Denis on our days off and gave examples of his wisdom and insight. With them, I grieved deeply and was angry that he had died without our permission and left us so suddenly.

My group at *Jesus Caritas* were shocked to hear that St. Vincent's parish was doing so well spiritually, educationally, and socially while at the same time its pastor felt so abandoned. I wrote an article for the diocesan newspaper *The Beacon* entitled "Loss of a Soul Friend." Writing the article was a catharsis for my sadness about Fr. Denis' death, and aided my grieving and healing. It was also a way of letting my many friends in Madison and throughout the tri-county diocese of Paterson know that this outwardly smiling, upbeat Irishman was hurting deeply on the inside. More than ever, I also relied on my prayer life.

During centering prayer in the little chapel, I would sometimes become so focused in discerning the will of God in my life that had the feeling of being outside of my body. I learned to appreciate the depth of God's love for me. I felt that, in spite of my human frailties, He would never give up loving me. He had a plan for me. My only responsibility was to listen to Him in prayer. After each visit to the chapel, I would return refreshed spiritually and emotionally to rejoin the St. Vincent's family that was growing spiritually, educationally, and socially.

On my way back from these sessions, I would frequently stop in at St. Vincent's School to get hugs from the first graders and to offer support to the fine principal. Some of the teachers, aware of my trips to Bethlehem Center, would tease me saying, "Children, look! Father Finbarr has a halo around his head." Ministering to the children helped me cope with the sense of loss I felt in not having my own family.

After we had celebrated Christmas and the New Year of 1985, members of the parish council suggested, "We would like to celebrate your Silver Jubilee as a priest. Since you have taught us how to really celebrate, we want it to be a party that everyone, especially you, will remember." There was no point in objecting even though I knew that they I was more at ease with giving than with receiving. I agreed, but only on the condition that the event celebrate the total parish and everything that we had achieved together.

The organizing committee proposed a children's celebration at the school on Friday, a Jubilee liturgy at twelve o'clock noon on Sunday, to be followed by an open house, and then followed by a Sunday afternoon liturgy with all of the bells and whistles. The weekend festivities were to culminate with a testimonial dinner dance early on Sunday evening. I insisted that the cost of the dinner be low enough to allow the average family to participate.

The Jubilee committee sent invitations to my family and friends in Ireland to join the festivities. They quickly received more than enough offers from parishioners who were eager to house and feed those of my Irish family and friends who would attend. My first big surprise was that our old nanny Mary Beatty was planning to make the trip (I was, after all, Mary Beatty's favorite baby). I did feel some guilt. Here I was, beginning to strongly doubt my longevity in the priesthood, and everyone else was expending great effort to celebrate it.

Meanwhile, Fr. Joe and Fr. Jim decided to host a priest-only Jubilee party. They asked me for a list of sixty or seventy priests who had supported my ministry over the past twenty-five years. They also told me to trust them and not to interfere with their plans. The event would not be only a solemn occasion of blessings, as the last line in the invitation teasingly hinted: ". . . or because you sympathize with us for having put up with him every day for six years . . . "

To my surprise, sixty-five priests responded that they would attend. When the time arrived, the venerable Vicar General, Msgr. Brestel, was one of the first to enter. Fr. Callaghan, one of my predecessors at St. Vincent's, arrived in an invalid's chair. I began to think that the party would be relatively sane. But after cocktails, a "priest" in a cassock suddenly appeared, seeming drunk as a lord. My first reaction was, "Oh my God, get him out of here." I didn't recognize him. He was, in fact, a comedian from another town dressed up in a cassock. The drunken Father proceeded to roast me on my many foibles, real and imagined, in my twenty-five years in the priesthood. He finished his soliloquy with, "Is it true, Father Finbarr, that you taught Dr. Ruth everything she knows about sex?" After the buffet dinner Fr. Jim presented each guest priest with a t-shirt to commemorate the evening's fun at my expense.

The theme of my homily at the Sunday liturgy event was on the value of individual growth in community. I thanked everyone for being part of my life and ministry. Referring to the Gospel passage, I claimed that any good fruit I had managed to produce was the result of their participation in the pruning. I referred to the ongoing pruning that I was experiencing as leader of a dynamic parish like St. Vincent's. I also included the story of when my mother said, "Finbarr, you are a wonderful young man. I believe you are going to do something special with your life when you grow up."

A silence in the congregation caused me to pause. I then looked down at Mary Beatty in the first row and said, "Isn't that true, Mary?" expecting her to say a simple "Yes." She shocked me and everyone else in church when she blurted out, "Your mom said that to all nine of you." People started to giggle, and I responded, "I feel she said it with more emphasis when she said it to me." The whole congregation roared.

I thanked God for loving parents and a supportive family, and for all the people who had touched my life. After Holy Communion, Fr. Joe introduced members of my family, read a papal blessing that the committee had requested from the Vatican, and then brought down the house by adding, "I don't know if I can talk about the pope and Dr. Ruth in the same paragraph, but here she is." Everybody gave Dr. Ruth a very warm reception. For Dr. Ruth, full of pride for me and respect for my ministry, the moment was a very happy one.

As the choir sang one of my favorite hymns, "I'm Blessed," we all processed from the church and continued the celebration in the school auditorium. I felt deeply loved and greatly excited, my adrenaline pumping so much that I felt I could have walked on water at that moment.

Ma Haag was the roaster at the dinner. The effects of the rectory fire had left him quite feeble, and he walked very slowly and with great pain up the stage steps. Those who didn't know him groaned as if to say, "Couldn't the committee get anybody better than an old cripple to speak at Father Finbarr's Silver Jubilee?"

They immediately changed their tune as he grabbed the microphone and spoke in a deep, stained-glass-window voice, saying, "Fellow hostages." He added, "Who would spend $25 to come on a nice Sunday afternoon here in Madison unless you were forced to be here?" He shared humorous stories of when we were stationed together and then spoke briefly of the rectory fire from which all three priests escaped. He finished by saying, "I have had forty assistants, but none of them could match Father Finbarr for hard work and dedication to his mission of caring for people." He concluded by saying, "I have never enjoyed any associate more than he. Unfortunately some of the things we discussed at the dining room table cannot be repeated here." He stopped suddenly.

Sharon, one of the outspoken members of our choir yelled, "Don't stop now, Monsignor, tell it all."

I was very touched by all of their love but felt quite guilty because I couldn't guarantee that they were going to have a "Father" Finbarr for the next twenty-five years. I had made the decision earlier that year that I would take a six-month sabbatical to discern my future in the priesthood. If I felt I couldn't or wouldn't keep my vow of celibacy, painful though it might be, I would resign the priesthood and earn my living as a layman. But those thoughts were put on hold while friends and I went on a Silver Jubilee trip to Ireland.

The trip was the grand finale of the Jubilee. My "Tour Award Program," conceived on the previous trip to Ireland, was now well perfected. The Mary Quinn award, granted to the biggest whiner each day, commemorated a woman from the first trip who had constantly complained about almost everything. As counterbalance, the daily Cinderella Award was for the kindest person. The most humorous occasion of that award was when two young ladies on the bus, realizing that old Mr. Flynn had run out of clean underwear, took his t-shirts and underpants and had them washed at the local laundromat. The Murphy Award honored the tour member who bought the dumbest souvenir on the trip.

Another beautiful sunny day greeted us when we arrived in Shannon and, within an hour of arrival, we were on the way up to Galway. On the west coast we stopped to see the Cliffs of Moher, a spectacular scene of one thousand feet of sheer rock rising straight up out of the Irish Sea. When we reached the Great Southern Hotel in Galway city, we readied for the evening's medieval banquet and entertainment. The next morning we headed west along the shores of Galway Bay, with a break for tea in the village of Spiddal, where Gaelic is still spoken.

I thanked God for the clear day as we stopped along the way to admire the Aran Islands across the bay. At Conemarra the group were amazed that this unspoiled area with vast stretches of bog land and heather-clad hills had survived without being covered with homes and factories. At Cong, I remembered *The Quiet Man*, the film we had always watched in New Jersey on St. Patrick's night and which had been filmed in Cong in 1952.

Then it was on to Our Lady's Shrine in Knock, County Mayo, a perennial pilgrimage stop on every Catholic tour of Ireland and one of the world's leading shrines. Tradition has it that the Blessed Virgin Mary appeared to several little girls there two hundred years ago. I arranged to say mass at the main altar of the shrine, where I reflected in my brief homily on the value of devotion to Mary the Mother of God. At the end of the mass, we circled the shrine as we said the rosary, a devotion that each visiting Catholic pilgrim there performs, often in the hope of a miracle.

We continued north to County Sligo, stopping at Tobernault Holy Well and Mass Rock. Crossing over the county boundaries, we arrived in County Donegal and stopped for lunch at the Beleek Pottery factory. There we admired the craftsmanship of the local workers in forming and decorating the clay to produce delicate porcelain masterpieces. At the beautiful seaside resort of Bundoran, we drove up to the Great Northern Hotel, situated on a golf course that straddled the whole peninsula. Although the town had lost some of its charm over the years, the hotel's magnificent elegance was the same as it was fifty years ago when my uncle Fr. Lawrence and other priests would stay for two weeks of golf by the sea. Since I had brought a few golf clubs along, I persuaded three of my friends on the tour to join me for nine holes while daylight lasted.

By this time, almost everyone was addicted to the brown wheaten bread unique in bed and breakfast Irish cuisine as part of a scrumptious breakfast of eggs, sausages and black pudding. One of the young nurses on our group pleaded, "Father Finbarr, would you please ask them to serve the beautiful brown bread?" I answered teasingly, "I'll get it for you, but don't complain to me when we get back to Madison about how much weight you have gained. Remember, this bread is a minute on your lips and forever on your hips."

Because the drive to Dublin was a long one, the tour guide Gerry and I entertained the group with stories from our own experiences in Ireland. I told a story about one of our dyslexic neighbors in Cavan who would say to his neighbors, "Come out to the pigsty. I want to show you to the pigs." Or when the same gentleman was told of his coming home late at night after playing cards at a neighbor's, he said, "I couldn't believe it when I came home last night at midnight. The kitchen door was in bed and Mary was wide open." After two hours of this spontaneous comedy, one of the ladies near the back of the bus said, "Would you two gentlemen give us a break for twenty minutes? My sides hurt too much from laughing."

As we drove north again, my eyes swelled with tears at memories of my parents from my previous tour to Ireland. This sadness quickly disappeared as I saw many of my family and several friends waiting on the lawn. Our bus wound its way through a nine-hole golf course to the tranquil setting of the Park Hotel in Virginia, County Cavan, where I was overwhelmed to learn that some old friends whom I had known in the 1970s had driven over one hundred miles to attend the Jubilee celebration that night. The O'Reillys from Belturbet, the Caffreys from Oldcastle, and the Breslins from Kells, all friends of mine for many years, joined Eilish and Dympna along with Colm and Fonsie.

I received a beautiful Waterford crystal decanter and engraved stand from the Shanaghy family. Kathleen Caffrey asked those present not to record her risqué rendition of "Amazing Grace." Her husband, Jim, however, didn't mind them taping his humorous and lengthy poem *Dan McGrew*. Fonsie again served as master of ceremonies and encouraged some of the tourists to join him in roasting their pastor. The next morning one of the octogenarians on our tour was slow to board the bus. Her older girlfriend said, "Maggie, what's up?" She replied, "I can't get my butt on the bus. We were out too late last night with that party animal Finbarr."

Heading south through the Wicklow Mountains, we visited the hand weavers' factory at Avoca. This industry, founded in 1723, is known worldwide for its soft tweeds. At the Waterford crystal factory we admired how the glass is blown and cut into masterpieces. I received much teasing about the Irish and their drinking when we visited the Old Middleton Distillery, which boasts the largest still in the world. In spite of all the travel, in Cork the younger folks were not tired and persuaded me to take them out to a singing pub. They all had a good laugh when a tall, handsome guitar player announced, "I am Finbarr Reilly. I want to welcome our friends from over the waters to Sean McCarthy's pub." I was not surprised that we met another Finbarr in Cork, as the name originated there with a sixth-century Irish monk named Finbarr. Even the Protestant cathedral was named St. Finbarr's.

At Blarney Castle I shared the story of the lady from Texas who was leaving from Shannon airport after visiting Ireland for the first time. Due to board the plane at any moment, she moaned, "I cannot go back to Texas and tell my folks that I didn't kiss the Blarney Stone." A caring young man at the Aer Lingus desk said, "Madam it is not necessary to actually kiss the stone to get the gift of blarney. All you have to do is kiss somebody who kissed it." She said, "That's great. How about kissing you?" The young man had to confess that, even though he had grown up just ten miles from the famous castle, he had never kissed the stone. He went on to say, "Sitting over there on the bench is Monsignor McNulty. He is the parish priest of that town. I am sure he has kissed it." The Texas lady was in seventh heaven and trotted over to the monsignor with her tale of woe. "Excuse me, Monsignor. I just can't go back to Texas without kissing either the Blarney Stone or someone who kissed it." He replied rather bluntly, "I'm sorry, my good lady. I only sat on it."

At Killarney, some of us enjoyed a boat ride on Lough Leane, the largest of Killarney's three lakes, while others simply walked and admired the views of the lake with the Kerry Mountains in the background. By this time some of our group noticed that the accent of the Kerry people was different from the very high-pitched accent of those from Cork. Asked how the accents could be so different in places just fifty miles apart, our guide Gerry answered with typical Irish humor, "It's just that the Kerry people have more charm."

After a dinner of fresh Kerry salmon, we all, senior citizens included, headed to Danny Mann's pub for a lively evening of Irish ballads. By now, the group had grown accustomed to the local Irish comedians who told good-natured jokes to their visitors. That evening the comedian was reading a supposed article from a Galway newspaper about a bus of New Jersey visitors who, directed by their guide, stopped along a country road to climb out on their knees into a field of rushes to search for leprechauns. Then he asked, "What is the registration number on your tour bus anyway?" When we stopped laughing, one of the visitors asked, "Sir, have you ever seen a leprechaun?" He answered with a straight face, "I haven't sir, but I know they are there."

The next morning some of us enjoyed a round of golf at Ballybunion, one of Ireland's most famous courses, while others toured the spectacular Ring of Kerry, a drive of one hundred miles with mountains on one side and the varied Atlantic coastline on the other. At one of the offshore islands, the group learned how the early Christian monks had survived there. In the town of Killarney that evening, some of the shoppers were fascinated by the signs in the shop windows, including one notice that announced "Ears pierced while you wait." As we bade farewell to our hosts at Shannon airport, the tour guide Gerry reminded us, "When you return, don't forget to bring Mary Quinn and Cinderella with you."

**Finbarr enjoys having his nieces
celebrate his return to Kells**

**Finbarr enjoying a game
of golf with Fr. Pat Scott,
friend since 1949**

Chapter 17

California

At the same time that President Jimmy Carter confessed to the world that he had committed adultery in his heart, I was beginning to admit to myself that even though I was not physically committing adultery, my thoughts and desires were not what you would expect from a celibate priest. I was fortunate that I didn't have to go through this struggle alone. For several years I had benefited from the guidance of a wonderful spiritual director, a Benedictine monk named Father Andrew Sullivan

Throughout this period I would increasingly end my centering prayer with a question: "What are you preparing me for? Whatever your will for me is, Jesus, I am prepared to follow." My ministry became more focused, and my homilies, especially at funerals, more effective. I still felt the sadness of the deaths of those family and friends I had loved, especially of those who had died at relatively young ages. Now when I stood in the pulpit after reading the Gospel for a funeral liturgy and gazed at the grieving family, I could truly understand and empathize with their loss.

Thanks to my spiritual director and the guidance of my priest support group, I was no longer afraid. When the personnel director of the Archdiocese of Newark invited me to interview for the position of Rector of the seminary at Seton Hall University, I quickly agreed to meet with the selection committee.

I was very relaxed and honest as I addressed questions about what I viewed as necessary to train

189

new priests effectively. I emphasized the importance of a holistic approach to the training of seminarians as good preachers, with emphasis on ritual and the canon law of the Church. I also emphasized the need for a more positive attitude toward human sexuality and celibacy, and that young seminarians should learn to appreciate their sexuality as God's gift to be integrated into their identity as men.

The body language of the lead interviewer told me that he was threatened by my suggested approach. He dismissed me cordially with, "Finbarr, we appreciate your time and interest in this position and will call you for another interview if necessary after we have interviewed all the candidates." I knew that he would blackball any further discussion about my being Rector of the seminary. But this didn't dampen my spirits, and I felt good that I had answered straightforwardly.

With my Silver Jubilee now over, I decided that the time for a sabbatical had come. My plan was to spend three months at the Vatican II Institute at St. Patrick's Seminary in Menlo Park, California, and then three months studying in Rome. A survey filled out by the pastoral team and the Parish Council had told me that I ranked high on leadership and people skills, but also that I needed updating in theology, Scripture, and preaching.

I wasn't embarrassed by the survey results because my resolution was that, if I was going to stay in the priesthood, I wanted to be the best priest I could be. Even though I had a master's degree in pastoral counseling and a doctorate in family life education, I knew that I had not kept up with the developments in theology and Scripture over the years. The Vatican II Institute would take care of that.

My spiritual advisor Father Andrew was very enthusiastic about my taking the sabbatical. In his view, only in a restful, prayerful atmosphere would I be able to discern something as vitally important as my future in the priesthood. The issue of continuing my priesthood in another denomination where I would be allowed to marry was very attractive at first, but I felt that for an Irish Catholic to join the "opposition" would be too big a pill for my family to swallow. I couldn't stand the thought of being rejected by my whole family.

I discussed the issue with a former priest, also of Irish descent, who had become a Lutheran minister in Rahway, New Jersey. I told him my life story and believe I gave an accurate spiritual, cultural, and emotion picture of myself. When I finished he said, "Finbarr, it is going to be extremely difficult for you - a successful, mature, and beloved pastor - to walk away from Roman Catholicism and to join another denomination. I recommend that you resign the priesthood and find a position as a marriage and family therapist. After you have been out for a time, I am certain that you will meet some fine lady and marry her. During this time you should do a study of the Episcopalians, Methodists, Lutherans, and other congregations. I believe these steps will be necessary for you to handle this monumental emotional problem." The advice seemed sound, and I stored the information away for future reference.

In the fall of 1985 I prepared the parish for my absence from St. Vincent's. As usual, the people of St. Vincent's were very supportive. The only thing they asked of me was my promise to return. I was nervous. I knew that I would worry about the St. Vincent's family, even though the parish would be in the capable hands of the Diocesan Chancellor.

The school was due to reopen after the Christmas vacation on the same day that I was due to start my 4,000-mile drive to San Diego. Because I couldn't bear the thought of packing and driving off while my darling school children were watching, I loaded my car on the evening before I was to leave, got up early, and drove out of the St. Vincent's parking lot while they were still asleep in their beds. Overcome with thoughts of loss and uncertainty, I was crying by the time I was fifteen miles from the rectory. Where would this new journey take me? I didn't know.

My plan was to drive 500 miles a day, with stops along the way to visit friends. My first stop was in Virginia to visit a woman who had participated in several of the Family Life Bureau trips before her transfer there to the city of Fairfax for a business promotion. I didn't explain my reasons for taking a sabbatical to her. She was a single, professional woman. Even though I had no sexual attraction for her, I didn't want any details I shared to be misunderstood by her as a sexual advance.

On the road again the next morning, I headed for Biloxi to attend a reunion of fellow graduates from St. Patrick's seminary in Carlow. It was a wonderful, affirming experience to see old friends whom I hadn't seen in twenty-five years. I inquired about two of the former seminarians who had been the rising stars of my class, and was shocked to learn that both had resigned from the priesthood to marry.

I was pleasantly surprised to learn that one of our very quiet prefects had become a bishop. One of my favorite professors from Carlow, Fr. P. J. Brophy, was our guest of honor for the three days and brought the worrisome news about St. Patrick's that the number of applicants for the priesthood was dropping radically, and that, to survive, the seminary might need to dramatically redefine the scope of its mission.

Apart from these worries, there were many light and humorous moments, much golf, and late nights of poker, as one might expect when 110 Irish-born priests are together to kick up their heels with colleagues for three or four days. Gerry Cleary of County Galway was elected president of the group's southern constituency. He reminded the group of the many times he had broken the rules in the seminary: solemn silence, 1,516 times; talking to juniors, 454 times; visiting other seminarians' room without permission, 642 times; not making his bed, 540 times. Gerry finished his monologue with the question, "Do you really want to elect me, with such a poor record, as your president and representative to Carlow?" The group howled with laughter, but kept Gerry in office.

My next stop was New Orleans, home of the Mardi Gras festival. There I wanted to visit a state trooper who had called me two years earlier to report that two of my former parishioners had died in a terrible car accident. The wife was a Catholic who had returned to religious practice after twenty years away from the Church. Her husband had converted to Catholicism when he saw her joy in her faith. They had become my good friends at St. Vincent's after she started attending the 6:30 mass each morning.

On the day they departed for their move to New Orleans, I gave her a single rose in plastic water container. She called me several times from the highway saying, "Sweetie, I miss you already." I replied, "The rose will wither but our love for you will always be there. See you in February." That was one of our last conversations. The next call was from the state trooper, who, following up after the accident to notify next of kin, had found only my name and number in the couple's telephone records.

The drive across the desert to San Antonio gave me the opportunity to pray and listen to the voice of Jesus as I drove along. When I crossed the border into the state of California, I noticed the lush vegetation and thousands of acres of wheat and vegetables. Obviously the government and people of California were to be complimented for their ingenuity in designing an irrigation system that changed a dry, arid desert into fruitful land.

After a visit with my sister Marie and some time with cousins in Montecito, I took the scenic Route 1 Coastal Highway to Menlo Park, where St. Patrick's seminary sat secluded on the outskirts of the city. I was reminded of St. Patrick's in Carlow, except that the Menlo Park St. Patrick's had ten acres of lawn and woods with many paths for reflective strolls. Several of the thirty-one priests registered for the course had already arrived. No one else was from New Jersey, but some of them had also been born in Ireland.

Even though the director, Father Gene, and his staff at the Institute were very welcoming and the other priests very friendly, settling in was difficult for me. I had my personal phone, but I wasn't receiving any phone calls. I began to feel abandoned. I found it a challenge to switch from ministering to thousands of people for twenty-five years to allowing other people to minister to me for three months. Since we were each assigned to a priest spiritual director and a priest therapist to assist in our renewal, I made an appointment with my therapist later in the week.

By the time of my session with him, I had a bleeding ulcer. When I reported how busy and involved I had been for twenty-five years, he simply said, "Finbarr, it is hard for you now to give up control of all these people and allow us here at the seminary to nurture you." Within two weeks' time I was much better, both physically and emotionally.

The weather in northern California is generally fine, except at times in winter. That January was no exception. The heavens seemed to open, and it rained for seven days and seven nights, causing mudslides along the picturesque Coastal Highway. Naturally, this caused a delay for the five or six golfers in our group, who were eager to play on some of the area's beautiful golf courses. When I sent home some articles for the parish bulletin back at St. Vincent's, I reported on the floods and the mud slides. Phyllis Gianonne, our faithful parish secretary, published my address and phone number and encouraged parishioners' letters and phone calls to the waterlogged pastor. I felt much comfort and support from the letters and calls that followed.

As with the great flood in the time of Noah, the rains subsided after seven days. We golfers set out on our expedition. The fairways were still very wet after several days of rain, so the golf carts were restricted to the asphalt paths. I drove my first shot two hundred yards down the fairway only to discover, when I reached the spot where it landed, that my ball had plugged three inches into the mud. I persuaded my three colleagues to switch to hurricane rules, which allow the golfer to lift his ball out of the mud on and off the fairway to clean it before taking his next shot.

Our class schedule at the Institute was light compared to what all of us had experienced as seminarians. We were told to consider this time away from assignments in parishes, seminaries, colleges, and chancery offices as a time for total renewal. Because priests were often overweight, we were also asked to evaluate ourselves physically. On the second day we were all weighed with our clothes and shoes on.

I couldn't believe that I was ten pounds heavier as a result of all the candy and junk food I had eaten during my ten-day drive from New Jersey. To encourage results, the director of the program set up a challenge. At the end of ten weeks, those priests who hadn't lost weight would treat those who were successful to dinner at a restaurant of choice. Naturally I loved the competition and had daily side bets of ten cents with the priest sitting to my right.

The most positive experience for all of us during our time at the Institute was exposure to the thinking of some of the best theologians and Scripture scholars in the United States. Fr. Osborne broadened our knowledge of moral theology but also gave us insights on how each of the seven sacraments was instituted. Some of us were surprised to learn that only two of the seven sacraments were actually instituted by Jesus. We weren't surprised to learn that the Church no longer held any belief in limbo, a supposed place on the edge of heaven or hell.

Fr. Ray Browne, recognized among Biblical scholars as the world's leading expert on St. John's Gospel, gave wonderful lectures on how each of the four Gospels was written, including details about which Gospel authors copied from others. During the past twenty-five years I had developed my knowledge of psychology and human sexuality. I learned the extent to which moral theology had evolved and how the discovery of the Dead Sea Scrolls had brought a renaissance in the understanding of the Bible.

Apart from the ten hours of class per week, there was little structure. We were encouraged to spend an hour in prayer daily and to take advantage of guidance from our spiritual director as we launched into spiritual renewal. The major reason for my taking a sabbatical had been to resolve my struggle over thirteen years. Could I, a very passionate Irish man, cope with the growing desire I had for a permanent relationship with a woman? Unfortunately, I had difficulty sharing these thoughts with the person assigned to be my spiritual director, who seemed very effeminate and no match for my regular spiritual director back in New Jersey. I did, however, take advantage of the hour's silence each morning to read my Divine Office and spend the rest of my time listening to the voice of Jesus speaking to me in prayer.

A great sense of fraternity and vulnerability developed among the priests. When one of the priests became very sick and we suspected he had AIDS, the group gave him comfort and support. Another priest admitted that he was homosexual in his orientation and shared with the rest of us how difficult it was for him to remain celibate. I shared my own struggles with celibacy with a few of the other priests. Everyone was very supportive and non-judgmental. One local priest who belonged to an order comforted me with, "Remember, if you resign the priesthood, that our Divine Lord loves you as much on the day you leave as the day you entered the priesthood."

To assist us in developing our skills as preachers, each of us chose a particular day on which we would be the principal celebrant and homilist for the community Mass. I chose March 19th, the feast of St. Joseph. I prepared a homily that began with the line "I never danced for my father," which was also the title of a Broadway play. I spoke briefly about my father as a quiet, hardworking farmer just as St. Joseph was a quiet, hardworking carpenter. None of St. Joseph's statements are recorded in the Scriptures, in spite of his awesome responsibility as the foster father of Jesus, Savior of the World. I tied in my remarks with the readings from Scripture and encouraged my congregation to emulate the virtues of St. Joseph. I drew smiles from all my colleagues when I concluded my homily with, "Would anybody like to dance?"

The experience of St. Patrick's, Menlo Park, had a dramatic influence on my life. The update in Scripture, theology, and liturgy restored my self-confidence as a priest. Looking at myself in a spiritual mirror, I could say honestly, "Finbarr, you are a good priest but you need to honestly address the issue of celibacy." For the first time it became clear to me that I really did have a vocation to the priesthood but that I didn't have the gift of celibacy. This was an issue I needed to resolve before I would resume my duties as pastor three months hence.

As with all good experiences, there is a beginning and an end. I wasn't looking forward to saying goodbye to all the good friends I had met at St. Patrick's. We treated each other as equals. I was not the only extrovert in the group of thirty-one priests. Several easily matched me in telling jokes and playing pranks. For the farewell party at a local restaurant, which I organized, a few of us did a parody on we had learned at the Institute, with some playful mimicking of Fr. Gene and his staff. We borrowed suitable costumes. I found a Scottish kilt, as I knew all would enjoy my interpretation of the Irish jig. A good time was had by all and the kidding taken in style.

My one mistake that night was losing track of how many glasses of wine I had consumed. Driving back, I was pulled over by a young policeman. Fortunately, I had changed out of my kilt. The policeman was not at all impressed that I was a pastor from New Jersey, as a policeman in the East might have been. Fortunately, I managed to walk a straight line, touch my nose, and recite the alphabet. I was very embarrassed to have police car lights swirling around my head after all my years of cautiousness about drinking.

The following morning I bade farewell to everyone, and, with only a brief stop back at the parish in Madison, was ready to head for Rome and the second part of my sabbatical adventure.

Chapter 18

Bella Roma!

My decision to stop in Madison on the way to Rome was a big mistake. From the moment I arrived, I was bombarded with nothing but problems. People had questions and comments about parish administration, which I couldn't criticize since I was technically not the administrator at that moment. There were problems with the school and the cemetery that weren't resolvable in two days. Others just said, "Father Finbarr, we miss you. When are you coming home to stay?" In the space of forty-eight hours I went from being totally calm and centered to feeling frustrated, angry, and selfish. Here I was, leaving again, this time to Rome to nurture myself spiritually and emotionally, while my flock missed me terribly. To top it all off I wasn't certain how long I would remain in the priesthood. This time I hid my true feelings.

I celebrated the 10:30 mass on Sunday morning and teased the choir that, after three months in Rome, I would come back singing like an Italian soprano. They didn't believe me, but the children who came up to me for a hug believed me when I said, "I love you and will miss you." I asked one little boy what he would like me to bring him. He said, "A Lamborghini sports car." Another parishioner asked, "Father Finbarr, would you please bring me back a Gucci handbag?" "Sure," I answered. Fr. Jim drove me to the airport and urged me not to worry about the parish, that all that everyone was really saying was that they had greatly missed me, especially since my temporary replacement as pastor had the personality of a wet dishrag.

The flight to Rome was uneventful. I should have been nervous since my knowledge of the Italian language was minimal. All I knew was that I had room and board reserved at *Casa del Clero* (House of Clerics) for the next three months. What I should have also realized, since there were thousands of clerics in Rome, was that there was more than one *Casa del Clero*. With help from a kind monsignor, I found my new home. I could tell by all the noise outside my bedroom window that I was in a heavily populated area. To add to the excitement that afternoon, Italy had just won a game against Germany in the World Soccer Cup.

The house director helped me get settled. He assured me that I would have no trouble with language, as there were already fifteen English priests in the residence. He also suggested that if I wanted to learn a little Italian, a tutor could come in for individual lessons twice each week. I was delighted at the opportunity to learn Italian, and looked forward to returning to Madison and saying a mass in the native tongue of some of my St. Vincent parishioners.

The next morning I invited myself to join the other priests in the residence to concelebrate mass. The little cardinal who was the chief celebrant looked very familiar. When I asked about him, one of the English priests smiled and replied, "He is the cardinal who announces "*Habemus Papa* (We have a pope)" from the balcony of St. Peter's when the rising white smoke gives the signal that the cardinals have elected a new pope." The little cardinal, noticing that I was a new visitor to *Casa de Clero*, greeted me warmly when he asked if I spoke any Italian. I confessed to him that I didn't, but that I was planning to have my first lesson with a tutor that afternoon.

Then he added, "Before you go back to America I want you to be the principal celebrant at the concelebrated mass here. Obviously you will celebrate the mass in Italian." I gladly accepted the challenge.

Casa del Clero was very centrally located, and the weather was perfect for walking. As usual, April and May in Rome were delightful that year: seventy degrees in the morning and eighty degrees during the middle of the day, with little humidity. It was only a three-minute walk to the very popular plaza *Piazza Navona*, which contained some of Rome's most beautiful statues and monuments. The walk along the Tiber River to St. Peter's Square and the Vatican took about fifteen minutes.

St. Peter's Square, about the size of a two-hundred-acre farm, was one of my first destinations. I wanted to enter it alone to experience all of the feelings of a cradle Catholic walking the holy ground where St. Peter had first established Christianity. It was late afternoon. The usual peddlers were hawking Pope John medals, souvenirs, and slides of the Vatican. A few cardinals in crimson red were leaving their offices to walk back to their residences, often accompanied by a young monsignor impeccably groomed in a fine black suit and Roman collar. In my few days of residence at *Casa del Clero*, I had become familiar with the young monsignors, several of whom were residing there.

The political picture I observed was one of bright young priests who had come from abroad to study in one of the Vatican colleges and then to obtain a job in one of the many Vatican offices, called *curia*. If they were lucky, one of the distinguished cardinals took them under his wing and became their mentor. I sat for an hour near the fountain to meditate. I decided that I was fortunate not to have the ambition to be a cardinal or a bishop and that this place, Rome, would be a restful place to discern my future in or out of the Catholic priesthood.

Fueled by my earlier studies of Latin and Spanish, I started my lessons in Italian three days after my arrival. The afternoon after my first class I ventured out to give my newfound language a test. I boarded a bus, where I struggled with asking directions while everyone on the bus listened. One young lady asked in Italian, "When did you start studying Italian?" I answered, in Italian, "*Ieri* (Yesterday)." Very welcoming and supportive even though I was murdering their beautiful language, the busload of Italians applauded and said in unison, "*Bello, bello* (Beautiful, beautiful)."

During my stay I planned to continue to pray for at least one hour per day and to find a temporary spiritual director. Other than attending courses on Christian archaeology and spirituality, I was free to visit Rome's galleries, museums, churches, and piazzas. My prayer life improved daily. After concelebrating mass early each morning, I went to the roof of our building, which had comfortable seating and a great view of St. Peter's Basilica and most of Rome. I was high enough not to be bothered by the busy city traffic, and I was usually alone except for one hungry pigeon and an old Italian priest who came daily to read his Divine Office.

One of the first people I met was a wonderful Jesuit priest, originally from India but relocated to Rome to teach spirituality to seminarians and priests. I shared with him the story of my spiritual journey and the history that, since my childhood, I had wanted to be a priest like my Uncle Fr. Michael. I also shared with him my successes and failures as a priest, and above all, the joy I felt in having served God and the Church unselfishly for twenty-five years. He was very affirming, telling me how fortunate I was to have so many of the gifts that were needed in Church leadership. He seemed disappointed when I added that I had no particular desire to advance to a higher office in the Church.

When I also shared that I was struggling with my vow of celibacy, he was not shocked. He simply said, "Finbarr, you are a very human and warm person. It is not unnatural for you to be attracted to women, and I am sure the women in America likewise find you attractive." I told him that one of my primary reasons for taking a sabbatical was to discern my future in the priesthood. I explained that I didn't want to be a hypocrite and continue in the priesthood if I could not promise to God and myself that I would be celibate for twenty-five more years. He was very quiet and reflective. Then I asked him, "Can you give me a good scriptural or theological reason for celibacy?"

He answered very solemnly, "Finbarr, there is no scriptural base or a good theological reason for celibacy. It is simply a Church discipline. It could change in time, but not during this pope's watch." The picture of what I needed to do was growing clearer all the time.

My new friends at *Casa del Clero* shared with me their assessment of the Vatican's Roman Curia and what they thought of the American Church. When I asked a French monsignor who had worked with Pope John Paul's predecessor, Paul VI, what this pope was really like, he smiled and said, "I am going to arrange for you and several of the priests who are on sabbatical here from England to say mass with him in his private chapel. Then I expect you as an American psychologist to give us an accurate assessment." I was very happy to have this honor, but I was not as excited as some of my English brethren. They were like kids in a candy store.

When the twelve of us arrived at the pope's private chapel the next morning, the pope was already there, dressed in white cassock and skull cap and praying on simple padded kneeler. There wasn't the slightest sound or distraction as we all prepared for this memorable mass. Just before nine o'clock, two nuns came from the back of the altar. Carrying the pope's alb, stole, and chasuble, his vestments for the mass, they dressed him.

For some strange reason, I was feeling quite detached and with little emotion. I wanted to pray the mass with the pope, and I also wanted to study him carefully up close. As the readings progressed, the pope was as intensely involved as if he was reading to himself. The Gospel story that day involved Peter's protestations to Jesus that others might deny Jesus but that Peter would never deny him. At the final five words, "He would never deny him," the pope actually shuddered. My interpretation of this response was that he himself would die rather than betray his role as Christ's Vicar on earth.

When the mass was over, the Vatican photographer took a picture of each of us guests shaking hands with the pope. As expected, Pope John Paul was warm and welcoming. Introducing myself I said, "Father Finbarr Corr, from Paterson, New Jersey." Handing me his usual gift of ivory rosary beads, he asked, "Is that far from Boston?" I answered, with an air of some surprise, "Only a few hours away, Holy Father."

As I walked back to our residence along the Tiber River, I realized that my impression of the pope had changed. When the French monsignor asked over dinner that night, "What does our American psychologist think of our Holy Father now?" I replied, "I learned a lot today. Before I had thought of him as an actor, like our television bishop back in the United States, Bishop Sheen, who loved to be in the limelight. Today I saw him as more like Gandhi, a lone ranger, who feels in his heart that it is his responsibility singularly to save Catholicism and that he has been appointed personally by Jesus to fulfill this task alone." The monsignor nodded his agreement.

I soon learned my way around by traveling on the bus, or walking and jogging from place to place. In the early morning quiet I jogged for two miles on the back streets to the Spanish Steps, a popular gathering place for tourists. On Sunday mornings I went to the American parish in Rome to concelebrate mass. On one of these occasions, the principal celebrant introduced all of us to the congregation, telling them where we were from and what was our purpose in spending time in Rome. I don't remember exactly how he introduced me but he must have presented me as somewhat of an orphan because a young Italian gentleman came up and said that his family would love to have me for dinner that evening. The young man's father was a director of Caritas, an international agency similar to our Catholic Charities back home, which ministered to the poor of the world and those suffering from AIDS. A second dinner guest was Archbishop Ferraioli, who had served many years as the Vatican's ambassador to Tanzania. Out of respect for the greenhorn from the United States, the group conversed in English, and all seemed to enjoy the stories I shared about the Church in America and my youth in Ireland.

At one of the social functions organized by several of the African students in Rome, I met Emanuel Milingo, an extraordinarily charismatic African bishop who had been in serious trouble with the Vatican not only for claiming to possess miraculous powers but also because he had introduced African culture and music into the liturgy in his diocese. During a private visit with Bishop Milingo, I shared my difficulties with mandatory celibacy and asked him if he felt the Church would ever lift the ban on married priests and women priests. He answered very quickly and also honestly, "Finbarr, it is eventually going to happen. We need it, particularly in third-world countries, but it is not going to happen while this pope is at the helm."

My conversational skills with Italian improved. I soon found myself able to converse with waiters in restaurants and the peddlers at the *Piazza Navona* and St. Peter's Square. During one of my language lessons, my Italian tutor discovered that I was a marriage counselor and began to discuss with me her marital difficulties and her impending divorce. She laughed when I commented that she should be paying me for counseling instead of being paid for tutoring me. Before I left Rome I made a final visit to *Piazza Navona*, where in my first days there I had spotted a painting of St. Peter's Square that the artist held for me until I had the money to pay for it. The deal was quickly made, and he packed the painting carefully for its transfer to New Jersey.

I packed a small backpack and took the train first to Florence, my favorite Italian city because of its museums and beautiful churches. The sculptures of Michelangelo and his colleagues attracted artists and art connoisseurs from around the world to *Bella Firenze* (Beautiful Florence). Traveling alone on the train with no particular timetable was usually a freeing experience. This time my stop in Venice was a blur because I was totally absorbed in what my journey would be all about once I returned to my post as pastor in Madison. Would I return fully determined to be a good, faithful and celibate priest? Or would I follow the dictates of my conscience and take another path to save my soul while still serving God in a different lifestyle?

After spending the night in Venice, I boarded the train again and headed towards Turin. The rest of my unplanned journey would be virgin territory to me. I had never been to Turin, home of the famous shroud with the sorrowful face of the crucified Jesus. Arriving in the late afternoon with no reservations for bed and board, I was lucky to find accommodations in a Benedictine monastery.

The day was the Fourth of July. According to the international newspaper *The Herald Tribune*, a great centenary celebration with fireworks around the Statue of Liberty in New York Harbor was scheduled. I expected the program to be reported live on Italian television, but I didn't anticipate the handicap. There was only one television set in the monastery, and the picture was in black and white. To add to my dilemma, only one of the nineteen monks in the abbey spoke English, and he was nearly blind. This was probably the only moment during my three months in Italy that I felt homesick for my adopted homeland America. As I said my nightly prayers, I thanked God for all the amenities that bless those who live in the United States. I also thanked Him for the freedom that Americans have but that many of them unfortunately take for granted.

I continued my pilgrimage across the north of Italy into southern France, visiting cities that I had read about in geography classes back at Legaginney School. I must confess that my class in Legaginney had never learned about the topless women bathers I witnessed on the beaches in Cannes and Nice. I wanted to spend a little extra time in Avignon, where popes had spent many years in exile from Rome. I continued my journey through Spain, stopping briefly in Madrid to make the one-day pilgrimage north on the narrow gauge railroad to visit the shrine of the black Madonna. A visit by any Irish Catholic to that part of the world would not be complete without continuing on to Our Lady's Shrine in Fatima, Portugal. It was to Fatima that Our Holy Father himself went on pilgrimage to thank our Blessed Mother for protecting him from the would-be assassin who attempted to take his life in St. Peter's Square. At Fatima I met some Americans and several fellow Irishmen who were reciting the rosary as they circled the beautiful basilica and prayed for miracles.

I had visited many shrines where Mary the Mother of Jesus was reported to have appeared to call the world to repentance. Many of these shrines, like Lourdes in France, had become very commercial, noisy places that discouraged contemplation and reflection. Fatima was quite the opposite. After saying mass in the basilica, I spent a full hour doing centering prayer, asking Mary to intercede for me with her Divine Son to reveal to me what was His will for me. At Fatima I understood what I would do when I returned as pastor in Madison. I would wait to see if someone with whom I wanted to spend the rest of my life came along. The decision was a liberating one. I was not making it for any particular woman because there was no such woman in my life at that time. As I took the train north from Fatima towards San Sebastian and the Moor country, I wondered if my decision at Fatima was the answer to my prayer for a miracle.

On the train north I met a Catholic priest and a seminarian from a very conservative order. The priest, dressed in a black cassock and with a pair of rosary beads hanging around his neck, had a difficult time believing that I was an American priest since I was dressed in a t-shirt and blue jeans. My agreement to join them for the rosary on the train that evening seemed to convince him. When we reached the city of Salamanca late that night, I was determined to get off the train even though I didn't have a place to stay. For years I had heard of the Irish seminary in Salamanca attended by aspiring priests from Ireland whose grades were too poor for admission to the Dublin seminary. These seminarians would study for six years in Spain and then return home to Ireland to be ordained.

The station was quite dark, and I was the only person getting off he train. Once again my Irish luck came to play. A middle-aged woman approached and asked me in Spanish if I needed a place to sleep. Without asking the cost, I said, "*Si* (Yes)." That night was a frightening experience. The woman showed me into a big room with six beds. Five of the beds already had occupants - men, I presumed. The woman took my passport, as is the custom. I could easily understand her paranoia. After an hour in the room, even I was strongly tempted to dress quickly and flee back to the station. The poor guy in the next bed must have been suffering from some awful chest or throat malady. He couldn't stop coughing and spitting up phlegm. Our four roommates seemed to be sleeping through the din.

After three hours of sleep, I arose at first light, paid five pesos, and retrieved my passport. I headed back to the station, where I was lucky to find George, an English-speaking taxi driver, to show me the town and the seminary. Because it was early summer, however, there weren't any students at the seminary. The priest in charge explained further that there hadn't been any Irish seminarians in the past ten years because of the declining number of vocations In Ireland.

I took George for a late breakfast and thanked him profusely as I boarded the train bound for San Sebastian, a beautiful seaside city that invites the traveler to linger. My landlords there were very hospitable and invited me to have Sunday dinner with the family at no extra cost. But I declined the offer and explained as graciously as I could that my brother Fonsie and his family were waiting in France for my arrival.

The ride out to the farm where Fonsie and his family were camped for the month of August was uneventful. I received the usual hugs and warm reception from all. For three days we swam in the ocean and played in the sand. Fonsie's daughters chastised their dad for staring at the French women who were running around topless. Their mother's look told me that I was not to encourage my brother's deviant behavior.

Late one night, as Fonsie and I were finishing a bottle of red wine, he surprised me by saying, "Finbarr, you are laughing and teasing as usual but your body language tells me that you are not your usual laidback self." I confessed, "Fonsie, you are correct, I am struggling to recommit myself to celibacy for the next twenty-five years. You can see that I am a family man, but I don't want to become a hypocrite like many priests, pretending to be celibate but having a girl on the side."

Fonsie gave me a big hug and said, "This has to be a more difficult decision for you than going into the seminary. Whatever you decide, you know I will support you. You were always there for me." Then, unable to resist a little humor, he added, "If you leave and marry, I suppose you will expect me to buy you some Waterford Crystal." Buoyed by his insight and acceptance, I took the overnight express to Rome, packed my few belongings, and headed for the airport and back to America.

Arrivedirce Roma!

Epilogue

With *Arrivederci Roma* ringing in my ears, I boarded my Alitalia Flight back to New Jersey to begin the final step of my sabbatical. When I arrived back in St. Vincent's, I realized just how much I had changed and grown in just six months. The three months in California had restored my confidence in myself as a preacher and had given me an updated and practical understanding of the New Testament and moral theology. The spiritual direction and counseling I received now helped me see myself from two different viewpoints. There was Finbarr the priest who loved God deeply, served Jesus his model unselfishly, and shared his talents in ministering with the thousands of people I met in churches, parish halls, during counseling sessions, and at Family Day rallies. The second Finbarr, the celibate priest, didn't get such a high mark. Difficult and as contradictory as it seemed, I had to admit that while I had a vocation to minister as a priest, I wasn't blessed with the gift of celibacy.

The three months in California renewed my belief in myself. The time in Italy proved to be a journey of liberation. I had traveled a dual highway, not knowing exactly where either road would lead me. The first highway involved a spiritual journey, going back to the origins of Christianity in Rome and seeing how the original message of Jesus to Peter and the apostles to "build My Church" had materialized into what one might call a great temporal empire. Still the kid from Legaginney, I had a hard time visualizing the simple message of Jesus to "feed My lambs and feed My sheep" carried out easily amidst the pomp and

213

ceremony in St. Peter's Square or in the rules and regulations spewing from the curia offices. While spiritual direction and my daily centering prayer helped me appreciate Jesus' love for me and its enduring quality, the opulence of the Vatican's architecture and paintings was a distraction in my spiritual journey. Through all of these religious experiences in Rome and at Our Lady's Shrine in Fatima, I learned to appreciate the difference between what is eternal and what is passing, between what is God's creation and what is man's. Through it all my faith in God and appreciation of Christ and His Church became deeper and stronger.

The second spiritual journey related to the issue of mandatory celibacy. When I reflected on my difficulties with celibacy over the past thirteen years and my determination to resolve the conflict one way or the other, I could now see only one final answer, "Finbarr, you must recognize that you don't want to be celibate or single for the next twenty-five plus years." As that response circled in my brain, all I could hear was, "How will my family accept my decision? Can my spiritual family back at St. Vincent's accept the fact? There will no longer be a Father Finbarr to hug their kids, to listen to and heal their wounds, and to create a family spirit for all eighteen hundred families. How will my bishop and the three hundred thousand people of the Paterson diocese, Catholics who know me at least by name if not through my actual ministry, accept my jumping ship after so many years as a leader of their flock?"

The captain of our Alitalia flight requested that the cabin crew should prepare for landing. I felt relieved that I had made the decision about my future in the priesthood. I was further relieved that I didn't have to share my decision with anyone except my spiritual director Fr. Sullivan. I knew what Andrew would say: "God will love you as much on the day you leave the priesthood as on the day you entered."

I received a very warm welcome back at all the masses on the first Sunday of August. No one yet realized that I was in a very vulnerable stage, both in my spiritual journey and in my life's journey, or that the end of the sabbatical marked a new beginning in my life.